S0-ARM-997

Classic

MALT

WHISKY

In the same series:

Classic Gin
  Geraldine Coates

Classic Vodka
  Nicholas Faith & Ian Wisniewski

Classic Tequila
  Ian Wisniewski

Classic Cocktails
  Salvatore Calabrese

Classic Stout and Porter
  Roger Protz

Classic Bottled Beers of the World
  Roger Protz

Classic Irish Whiskey
  Jim Murray

Classic Bourbon, Tennessee and Rye Whiskey
  Jim Murray

Classic Blended Scotch
  Jim Murray

Classic Rum
  Julie Arkell

Classic Brandy
  Nicholas Faith

Classic
MALT
WHISKY

Ian Wisniewski

First published in 2001 in Great Britain by
Prion Books Limited
Imperial Works
Perren Street
London NW5 3ED
www.prionbooks.co.uk

A CIP record for this book is available from the
British Library

ISBN 1-85375-413-7

Printed and bound in China by Everbest

CONTENTS

INTRODUCTION
3

CHAPTER ONE
MALT WHISKY'S HISTORIC PROGRESS
6

CHAPTER TWO
ISLAY & PAGODA ROOFS
16

CHAPTER THREE
MAKING MALT WHISKY
22

CHAPTER FOUR
BRAND DIRECTORY
92

CHAPTER FIVE
MALT WHISKY CULTURE
150

GAZETTEER
175

INTRODUCTION

I knew there would be a lot to learn, but the distillers I met while researching this book proved to be more like mentors than interviewees. Instead of reciting the unique selling points of their brands, they were intent on explaining the art of producing malt whisky, and readily shared their expertise with me.

While visiting distilleries, I generally had a notebook or glass in my hands, though I also gained some hands-on experience. At Bowmore Distillery on Islay, I tried cutting peat (a job I would never get), as well as turning the barley on the malting floor. As this entailed dragging a 'plough' behind me, it was far more demanding than my usual 30 minutes on an elliptical fitness crosstrainer.

In fact, every trip yielded 'firsts' of some kind. At The Macallan, I learned about Golden Promise, a significant variety of barley, and had my first taste of the new make spirit it yields, fresh from the still. At The Balvenie, I sampled numerous vintages of malt whisky straight from the cask, while snow lay six inches deep outside the aging warehouse. At Talisker on the Isle of Skye, I saw my first worm tub (great

Opposite
*The river
Sligachan on
the Isle of Skye.*

3

excitement!), and watching Edradour's antique accessories in action was a masterclass in tradition.

How a national spirit evolved, how it is served, and the traditions surrounding it, are just as important to me as the production methods involved. This is why I have dedicated a chapter to malt whisky's essential role in Scottish social life and hospitality; some of which I was able to experience. My debut *ceilidh* at Glen Grant, was a great evening, with live music courtesy of an accordion and a fiddle. I love dancing, and did my best to strip the willow, (although my forté is really freestyle).

Visiting Highland Park, I learned about various traditions exclusive to Orkney. I was six months too early for the annual malt-fuelled, New Year's day football match known as The Ba', but strolling by the sea with a glass of malt, under the extraordinary midnight light of midsummer, provided my own personal Orkney Event.

Having already developed a deep commitment to fruitier, creamier styles of malt whisky, I assumed I would have the peaty, smokey numbers to look forward to as my palate matures. By the time I'd finished writing this book that had already happened, so I'm delighted to be ahead of schedule.

Producing malt whisky is, in one sense, a straightforward process. Barley is malted, milled and mashed, which yields a sugarey liquid fermented by adding yeast. This is distilled twice in copper pot stills and aged in oak barrels. However, every step of the process offers numerous options, all of which can exert a profound influence on the resulting whisky, and on the people who drink it.

"Friar Royd"
FINE OLD SCOTCH WHISKY
JAMES H. FRIAR ROYD SCOTCH WHISKY LONDON & GLASGOW
JAMES H. S. HOLROYD,
19. St DUNSTAN'S HILL. LONDON. E.C. AND AT GLASGOW

MALT WHISKY'S HISTORIC PROGRESS

THE SHORT VERSION

How the knowledge of distillation reached Scotland is not as important as how the Scots subsequently elevated it into an art form. Monasteries were the earliest centres of distillation, and the knowledge may have been passed on by the monks who introduced Christianity from Ireland, with St Columba and his nephew St Drostan founding the first monastic cell in Scotland during the 7th century. Monks had in turn acquired the principles from China and the Ancient Egyptians, who distilled flowers and plants to produce perfume.

As Highland farmers began distilling beer produced from surplus grain (beer being one of the earliest alcoholic drinks), the result was a prototype whisky. This was called *uisge beatha* or *usquebaugh*, Gaelic for 'water of life', which alternated with the Latin term *aqua vitae*, also meaning 'water of life'. This reflected a belief that drinking whisky promoted youthfulness and longevity. The earliest reference to 'whisky' dates from 1494, with the Scottish Exchequer Rolls referring to 'eight bolls of malt to Friar John Cor wherewith to make aqua

Opposite
Monasteries were the earliest centres of distillation.

vitae.' A boll is a historic Scottish measure: eight bolls are sufficient to distill around 1,500 bottles.

In 1644, the first Excise Act was passed, setting the level of duty on malt whisky. As distillation was practised on remote farms, using small, portable stills that were easily concealed, no one was willing to pay unless caught in the act.

It was a different story for the earliest commercial distillery, Ferintosh, which was established by Duncan Forbes of Culloden and first referred to in the 1690 Acts of the Scottish Parliament. The Act of Union in 1707, which united England and Scotland, also imposed a medley of excise rates and regulations on the patriotic, whisky loving population. An early 18th-century Jacobite slogan said it all: 'No union, no salt tax, no malt tax.' Moreover, malt whisky was already an integral element of social life. As an 18th-century Highland lady noted, 'At every house whisky was offered, at every house it must be tasted or offence would be given ... Decent gentle-women ... always began the day with a dram.' The English regime soon began to implement more stringent taxes and duty, not only to extract revenue, but as a means of repressing Highland customs and nationalism. However, by the end of the 18th century, fewer than ten distilleries were licensed; but thousands more, throughout Scotland, were unlicensed and virtually unstoppable.

Orkney, originally a Viking kingdom and part of Scotland from 1471, was a prime example. Its most accomplished smuggler was Magnus Eunson, who worked an illicit still from 1798. This was a sideline to his preaching at the local Kirk, although he combined both occupations by stashing illicit whisky beneath his pulpit. When excise officers came into the church, he simply deflected any suspicion by delivering sermons with added gusto.

It wasn't only in remoter areas that illicit whisky was brisk business, and malt was regularly smuggled into Glasgow from the surrounding area. The couriers were young girls and their lady-like method of smuggling was to secrete tin pots full of whisky under the hoops of their skirts.

One of the most renowned centres of illicit distilling was Glenlivet in Speyside, where

Right
In 1777 there were 400 illicit stills in Scotland, compared to the 8 licensed distilleries.

remote farmsteads were a natural habitat for black marketeers. It was an equal opportunity occupation: women operated the stills, while armed men escorted ponies loaded with whisky along remote tracks, that were hopefully unknown to the excisemen. The local landlord, the Duke of Gordon, campaigned for reforms that would make distilling whisky profitable and so encourage legal production. This resulted in the 1823 Excise Act, which set a standard rate of excise and an annual licence fee of £10, as well as harsher penalties for illicit distillers.

The first of the Duke's tenants to take out a licence was George Smith, who founded the Glenlivet distillery in 1824. But it wasn't an example that others wished to follow. In fact, the other distillers were outraged and threatened to burn down his distillery. Nevertheless, it was the beginning of a new, legitimate era.

During the 19th century, a number of eminent whisky houses emerged. Some originated as grocers, selling their own malt whisky from a cask, with customers bringing empty bottles to the shop. As the quality varied, grocers who developed blending skills – combining malts of different ages and from various distilleries – soon stood out from the crowd. John Walker, for example, became the manager of a grocery

Below

Illicit whisky from the Glenlivet area long enjoyed an enviable reputation, with The Glenlivet the first to be licensed in 1824.

business in Kilmarnock in 1820. His son Alexander took over in 1857, and began to refine his blending as well as his marketing expertise, developing what became the Johnnie Walker brand of blended whisky.

Similarly, James Chivas, a farmer's son who joined a grocery business in Aberdeen in 1836, soon began blending whiskies for customers, and not just any old customers. He gained a Royal Warrant from Queen Victoria in 1843, a year after her first visit to Scotland, when she acquired a taste for a wee dram in her cup of tea.

Queen Victoria was also instrumental in popularising the Scottish Highlands among the English. She first stayed at Balmoral Castle in 1848, and numerous English aristocrats wishing to emulate their leader, began building castles and shooting lodges in the Highlands. They were introduced to the local speciality while hunting, shooting and fishing. However, malt whisky was pronounced overpowering by English palates brought up on a staple diet of French brandy. Grocers therefore began blending malt with lighter grain whiskies for a more subtle alternative. Blended whisky found its apotheosis in the form of 'Scotch and soda', which soon replaced brandy and soda. This was particularly important as stocks of brandy began to diminish during the 1870s, once phylloxera, a vicious insect, had devoured numerous French vineyards.

ANNO QUARTO

GEORGII IV. REGIS.

•••

C A P. XCIV.

An Act to grant certain Duties of Excise upon Spirits distilled from Corn or Grain in *Scotland* and *Ireland*, and upon Licences for Stills for making such Spirits; and to provide for the better collecting and securing such Duties, and for the warehousing of such Spirits without Payment of Duty. [18th *July* 1823.]

Left
Whisky
legislation
from the early
nineteenth
century.

As the English and other nationalities drank Scotch whisky more regularly, exports accelerated. By the beginning of the 20th century, Scotch was established as the world's leading style of whisky, ahead of the traditional champion, Irish whiskey.

The quality of Scotch was raised further when a minimum aging period of two years was established by The Immature Spirits Act in 1915. This was then extended to three years in 1916. However, as this act initially reduced the level of Scotch whisky on the market, it was in fact a mild form of prohibitionism, which the prime minister Lloyd George had intended.

When prohibition was established in the USA from 1919-33, preventing the production, importation and retail of alcohol, the key export market for Scotch whisky suddenly vanished. Exports to the USA revived following the repeal of Prohibition, but this only lasted until the outbreak of World War II.

Until the 1950s, many distilleries owned farms that supplied either some or all of their barley. They therefore operated seasonally (October to May), following the barley harvest. In the interim, employees either switched to farm work or undertook general maintenance at the distillery.

While malt whisky had been reserved almost exclusively for blends, with Scotland essentially the only market for single malts, Glenfiddich became an international ambassador for the category when first exported in 1963. However, it wasn't until the 1980s that malt whisky began to emerge as a global contendor, when more malts were marketed as a solution to the 'whisky loch', a vast surplus of malt and grain whiskies.

Around 85 malt whisky distilleries are currently operational in Scotland, with continual acquisitions resulting in a large number of brands becoming concentrated in the portfolios of a few multinationals. Technology enables some distilleries to be run by only a couple of men, making this the age of pcs and PLCs. However, distilling is not an automated, industrial process, and the real benefit of computers is being able to monitor every detail and temperature change as it happens. Despite technological advances, there is still a degree of mystique involved, as defining exactly how and why a certain approach yields the best result can still be difficult, if not impossible, to determine scientifically. And while the distillery workforce has decreased, increased marketing departments are working overtime in order to continue developing malt whisky's international cult status.

ISLAY

Fondly referred to as the Queen of the Hebrides, Islay is the most southerly Hebridean island. But that's hardly the most important superlative for an island that also yields some ultimate malt whiskies.

Making the most of the abundant peat moors and the marine air which permeates the aging warehouses, Islay's malts thrive on varying degrees of smokey, peaty and sea spray characteristics, enhanced by vanilla, fruity, citrus and malty notes. From a historic peak of 21 distilleries, the current line-up includes Ardbeg, Bowmore, Bruichladdich, Bunnhabhain, Caol Ila, Lagavulin and Laphroaig.

Islay is also home to about 3,300 people, not to mention thousands of geese, who take off from Iceland to spend the winter there. The temperate climate enables grass to grow throughout the winter, ensuring a staple diet for the geese. It's not surprising that numerous types of wildlife are drawn to the island, as its heather moorlands provide ideal nesting areas for various birds, with golden eagles, peregrines and merlins making an ocassional appearance. Turtles, grey seals and otters frolic on the beaches, sand banks and rocky coastline, while the island's restaurants provide another natural habitat for local lobsters.

Opposite
Sunset on Islay, often referred to as the Queen of the Hebrides.

In addition to Islay's rugged, romantic beauty, the town of Bowmore features an unusual 18th-century Round Church. Locals explain its shape as a strategic design feature, that avoids any corner in which the devil could hide. The 9th-century Kildalton Cross standing by the Ardbeg distillery, is one of the most impressive and historic examples of sacral art in Scotland: a legacy of the monks who fled from the marauding Norsemen on Iona.

Below
Bowmore's
Round Church
on Islay was
built in 1769
on top of the
hill on the edge
of the town.

Across a narrow stretch of water, known as the Sound of Islay, is the neighbouring island of Jura, whose dramatic mountains known as the Paps, provide a contrast to Islay's gentler undulations. Meaning 'deer island' in Old Norse, Jura's red deer vastly outnumber the human population, although a significant local resident is the Isle of Jura distillery.

PAGODA ROOFS

The pagoda roofs, which are such a feature of malt whisky distilleries, blend aestheticism with practicality, by drawing smoke from the malt kiln in the most efficient and stylish manner.

The genius responsible for this design, originally known as Doig's Ventilator, is Charles Chree Doig (1855-1918). Based on a classic formula used by the Ancient Egyptians to construct pyramids, it incorporated the height and width of the roof, together with louvred sections. However, for someone whose work was so celebrated, Doig left very little information about himself and the source of his inspirations. Burning all his diaries before he died didn't help.

The essential facts are that he was born into a farming family in Lintrathn, Angus. He joined an architectural firm in Elgin as a partner, before establishing his own business there in 1890. As Elgin was an important town in Speyside and the source of some superior malt whiskies, it was inevitable that Doig's client list would include distilleries, particularly as whisky exports soared from the 1880s. Meanwhile, he also worked on 1,200 other projects in the Elgin area, including townhouses, hotels and churches.

The pagoda roof originated in 1889 when Doig was commissioned by the Daluaine Distillery to replace an existing 'beehive-style'

chimney, which was not drawing smoke efficiently. Removing some of the chimney's numerous slats provided an immediate improvement, and the evolution of the pagoda design can be seen in his original drawings: an initial conical shape resembling a 'Chinese hat' became more curvaceous in a subsequent design, and evolved into a pagoda during the next draft.

What inspired the pagoda shape is open to speculation; it may have been the late Victorian vogue for chinoiserie. But whatever the source of his inspiration, it was soon clear where the genre was heading: all the way to the top with numerous distilleries queueing up for the Doig treatment. He also designed 23 entire distilleries, sometimes including the distillation equipment, as well as being involved in a further 100 distilleries. These included Cardhu, Glen Elgin, Highland Park, Imperial, Knockando, Longmorn, Strathisla and Talisker.

Where Doig led, other architects followed, and not all the pagoda-style roofs which can now be seen are his work, even some kilns used to smoke herrings and salmon adopted the pagoda look. While the pagoda design received all the credit for improving the flow of smoke, it was essentially a decorative feature. Raising the height of the chimney was the key element in improving the chimney's 'draw'.

An impressive collection of around 3,000 of Doig's original distillery designs have survived, and are kept in the archives at Elgin Library. Alternatively, there are more than 50 surviving examples of pagoda roofs which can be seen at distilleries throughout Scotland.

Opposite
Strathisla distillery in Keith, Banffshire was established in 1786 and lays claim to being the oldest distillery in the Highlands.

HOW MALT WHISKY IS MADE

BARLEY

Malt whisky is produced from barley cultivated in Scotland, essentially the Borders, Fife and Aberdeenshire, as well as England (principally Northumbria). Distillers can choose from numerous varieties of barley, particularly as more cost-effective and disease resistant varieties are continually being developed. While it can take six to ten years to commercialise new varieties (a result of team work between various institutions and plant breeders), they don't spend long in the fast lane, being overtaken every three to five years by even newer varieties.

Chariot, for example, accounted for up to 40–45 per cent of the market in the mid-1990s. This level of prominence had not been achieved since the heyday of Golden Promise, which was number one from the mid-1960s to the mid-1980s. But Chariot was soon supplanted. The year 2000 saw Optic become the leading variety, taking around 30 per cent of the market, with a host of other young pretenders also claiming their share.

The main varieties of barley currently being used, including Optic, Chariot, Prisma, Delibes and Chalice, were developed in the 1990s, and

Opposite
Inspiring, bold
  John Barleycorn
What dangers
  canst thou
  make us scorn.
Robert Burns

featured on the Institute of Brewing's 1999/2000 list of approved varieties for Scotland. The Institute promotes technical knowledge of the brewing and distilling industries, and includes a barley committee that assesses new varieties for distillation and brewing.

An initial difference between barley varieties concerns farmers as much as distillers, based on varying yields. For example, an acre planted with Golden Promise yields about two tons of barley, compared to Chariot and Tankard which yields around three tons per acre, and also ripens faster than Golden Promise.

However, it is the yield of alcohol that has really driven the development of new varieties. Chariot and Tankard, for instance, yield 420–430 litres of

Below

Barley used to distill malt whisky is principally grown in Fife and Aberdeenshire.

alcohol per ton, compared to Golden Promise at 380–395 litres, which is also around 20 per cent more expensive than other varieties.

Whether different barley varieties offer individual aromas and flavours beyond the generic range of cereal, bready and biscuity notes, depends on who you ask. 'No' is a frequent response, although even these distillers are unlikely to change barley varieties in the midst of a production cycle, in case it affected consistency.

Fortunately some distillers do believe in varietal differences, which means there is a debate to be had. Golden Promise, for instance, yields a rounder-bodied, oily spirit according to The Macallan, even though this variety only accounts for 30 per cent of the total amount of barley used at the distillery – the balance is Chariot. However, The Macallan used 100 per cent Golden Promise until the early 1990s and returned to these proportions in the year 2000. This yielded new make spirit with an oiliness considered to promote longevity and a better balanced whisky. Whether The Macallan will continue to use 100 per cent Golden Promise remains to be seen, as does the effect on the resulting spirit. Meanwhile, contracts with farmers ensure The Macallan's continued supply of Golden Promise. The distillery has also cultivated 300 acres of this variety on the estate since 1996, with plans to become organic. The Glengoyne is another distillery using Golden Promise in conjunction

Above
A field of Golden Promise barley near The Macallan distillery.

with Chariot, citing longer aging potential and a fruity, appley note on maturity.

Fans of the Melanie variety also claim it yields finer quality spirit. This is a variety of winter barley, which is sown in late autumn or early winter and harvested in July and August. However, most distilleries use varieties of spring barley, which are sown in the Spring and harvested in September. Melanie's alleged superiority reflects winter barley's higher level of nitrogen, which in turn influences the flavour compounds in the resulting spirit. However, a higher nitrogen level also means a lower starch level, which entails a lower yield of alcohol than spring barley.

Whatever the variety, once harvested, the barley

is stored during its 'dormancy' period, a schedule imposed by Nature to prevent the grains from germinating too soon. As barley can only be prepared for distillation once it is ready to germinate, the dormancy period is a relevant factor in the choice of barley. Newer varieties can also offer an advantage here: a variety developed in the 1990s germinates readily within four to six weeks, compared to a more historic variety like Triumph, which can remain dormant for up to three months.

To ensure barley emerges from the dormancy period, appropriate storage is essential. The barley is initially dried using hot air to a moisture level of below 15 per cent, when it can be stored in watertight conditions for up to a year or longer. However, it is essentially supply and demand that determines the length of storage.

STEEPING

The process of steeping prepares the barley for germination, by soaking it in tanks of fresh spring water. The water source used, particularly if it permeated through peat, can influence the eventual flavour of the whisky.

The water temperature is around 16–17°C in summer, and 18–20°C in winter, helping to soften the barley and facilitate the absorption of water. Tanks are drained and refilled with fresh spring water every 8–12 hours, during a total

steeping time of around 36–48 hours. A standard proceedure is to include a pause between refilling the tanks, pumping in oxygen to promote germination and help prevent grains from sticking together and rotting.

Once drained from the steeping tanks, barley is taken to the malting floor to germinate, the traditional mode of transport being a barrow or chariot. Usually an entirely wooden wheelbarrow is used to avoid any rusting, which could affect the barley. Modern versions include galvanised steel sections.

Some distillers claim a stone floor is best for germination, as it helps control the temperature better, and is less vulnerable to forming algae that may be detrimental to the barley. Some are in favour of cement due to its ease of cleaning.

Barley is spread evenly across the malting floor

and, being wet and warm, is set to do what comes naturally – germinate. During this stage the barley seed 'awakens' and begins secreting a combination of enzymes known as diastase, which break down the starch and proteins in the barley, making them soluble. This is the essential preparatory stage for converting the starch into sugar during mashing.

The length of time the barley remains on the malting floor also reflects the ambient temperature, and can be five days during the summer and seven in the winter. The objective is for the barley to germinate but not actually grow. Consequently it is 'turned' every few hours using a 'malt shiel' (spade), to redistribute it on the malting floor. Aerating the barley in this manner helps control the temperature and the rate of germination. An alternative is to use a machine

Below
Ploughing the barley to aerate it.

resembling a garden rotivator, or a three-pronged rake known as a plough. Another form of temperature control is thoroughly low-tech: simply opening or closing windows.

According to tradition, germination is stopped when the acrospire (shoot), and rootlet are no longer than the grain. Otherwise the grain will use up starch to continue growing, whereas the distiller requires a maximum starch content. Germination is arrested by drying the barley in a process known as kilning, reducing the moisture level from 40–45 per cent to 4.5–5 per cent. The kiln is fired by various types of fuel such as coke, and depending on the style of malt whisky being produced, peat is also added. Smoke rising from the fire passes through a wire mesh floor on which the barley is spread out. This process gives rise to an additional range of malt flavour compounds, while also developing the barley's existing range of flavours. Raising the heat and duration of kilning also increases the range of these malt flavours, but the temperature must be carefully controlled to preserve the enzymes within the barley, which are essential for the subsequent conversion of starch into sugar.

If peat is used, this is when the distinctive 'peat reek' is imparted to the barley. Peat smoke adheres to the exterior of the grain without affecting the interior. The level of peating is measured as 'parts per million phenol'. A lightly peated malt may have a total of two parts per million phenol,

with more distinctly peated malts at 30 and 40 parts, up to a peak of around 50 parts per million for the most heavily peated malts.

Peating time varies from around 16 hours, with the barley absorbing as much smoke as it can after about 24 hours. An established formula sees specific amounts of peat added to the fire at regular intervals to ensure consistency.

Peat also needs to be prepared prior to kilning. It can be either machine extracted, which tends to be more compact and burn more slowly, or hand cut, which contains a higher level of root matter.

Above
Kilns are
used to dry
the barley.

Hand cutting entails working in parallel lines several feet wide, across a moor. The top layer of turf, several inches deep, is removed, and is placed on top of the adjacent line which has already been worked. This ensures that the peat regenerates. Peat is extracted in two stages to a total depth of around four feet. The peat cutter (or peat spade), comprises a long teak or oak pole, sometimes accessorised with a cow's horn at the end to facilitate the grip. A narrow blade at the other end features a small 'wing' to aid manoeuvrability.

Each individual extraction results in a piece of peat around two feet long and six inches wide. The first cut of peat includes the root matter of

Right
Extracting the peat to prepare it for kilning.

plants such as heather, bog myrtle, mosses and various grasses. After extracting this first layer across the width of the line being worked, the peat cutter repeats the process on the underlying peat that has been exposed. This second, deeper cut of peat is much darker and oilier. Every six inches of peat below the surface is thought to represent 1,000 years, comprising pine trees and other forms of decomposed vegetation.

Freshly cut peat can only be handled using a peat cutter (involving a skilled balancing act), reflecting a moisture level of around 80 per cent, and is laid on the adjacent turf to dry. Within two weeks, a skin forms on the surface that prevents the peat from absorbing any rainfall as it continues to dry in the open. This skin also enables the peat to be handled. Peat is subsequently 'fitted' (stacked), for around four weeks in stooks, which are like a small wigwam or tower. Each piece of peat is placed so that the wet side (which lay on the turf), faces outwards. This promotes thorough drying to a moisture level of 5–10 per cent. Some distilleries also use a proportion of 'wet' peat, collected when it reaches a moisture level of 10–15 per cent, which produces more smoke than 'dry' peat.

Peat can also offer characteristics reflecting local influences. Highland Park, for example, uses peat from the distillery's own fields on Orkney, which has absorbed a certain degree of sea spray. Similarly, Islay peat, used by distilleries such as Bowmore, has a significant level of seaweed in

BENRIACH MALTINGS

addition to sea spray influences, resulting in a lightly oily peat with iodine, medicinal notes.

However, the vast majority of malting is now undertaken by commercial maltsters rather than individual distilleries, with The Balvenie, Bowmore, Highland Park, Laphroaig, and Springbank among the minority retaining their malting floors.

Commercial maltsters date from the 19th century, but only began to offer distilleries a more cost-effective package from the late 1950s and early 1960s. This resulted in many distilleries closing their malting floors in the 1960–70s. Maltsters operate on a large scale and typically use drum maltings which resemble vast tumble driers, in place of a malting floor. This is an entirely mechanised process, with air at selected temperatures blown through the germinating grain, which is turned automatically. The barley is malted according to each distillery's individual specifications, including the level of peating.

Once peating is concluded, the barley still needs further drying. This can be done by using either hot air or adding fuel such as coke or anthracite to the fire, with kilning taking a total of around 25–40 hours.

Once malted, the barley is stored for around four to six weeks. This improves fermentability and the subsequent yield of alcohol by allowing the remaining moisture to extend back throughout the grains, having been 'pushed out' to the edges by the heat during kilning.

MILLING THE MALTED BARLEY

En route to the milling machine, malted barley passes through the dresser. This catches any rootlets or extraneous items such as small stones,

which are not only undesirable but can damage the rollers of the milling machine.

The first set of rollers of the milling machine squeezes the grains to pop the husk, while the second set grinds the kernels further. This yields three separate grades of malt: husk, grits (or middles) which are medium-ground, and the much finer ground flour (or fines), collectively called grist. The typical specification is 20 per cent husk, 70 per cent grits and 10 per cent flour. This provides an ideal total surface area and enables the maximum amount of sugar to be extracted within the minimum amount of time during the subsequent mashing process, (which involves adding hot water to the grist to convert the starches into sugar). The proportions of each grade also reflect practical considerations. Husks help water drain through the grist, although too much husk would prevent the grist from mashing properly. Similarly, too high a level of flour can result in the equivalent of porridge.

Opposite
Milling the malted barley at Aberlour.

MASHING

The grist is combined with hot water immediately before entering a large vessel known as the mash tun. This is equipped with rotating arms that agitate the mash (grist and water) distributing water more evenly and ensuring a better rate of conversion from starch into sugar. The water drains through perforated metal plates at the bottom of the mash tun. Most distillers add two further sets of water, which are sprayed on from pipes under the lid of the mash tun. Many distillers claim that the spring water used can influence the eventual flavour, particularly if it has permeated through peat. However, at this stage it's the temperature rather than the source of the water that is crucial.

When the first water hits the grist, at 63–64°C, the enzymes created during malting begin converting starch into fermentable sugars. This water carries the highest level of fermentable sugars.

The second water at around 65–74°C helps to push through the first water, while also flushing out stickier sugars and instigating additional enzymatic reactions. These two sets of water, yielding what is known as wort, result in around

90 per cent of the starches within the mash being converted in the mash tun. Some unconverted starches also drain through within the wort, undergoing 'secondary conversion' as enzymes in the wort continue the process *en route* to the washback, where fermentation takes place.

A third water is added at around 85–90°C or even higher, but below boiling point which would otherwise damage remaining enzymes. This water washes out any residual sugars. Known as 'sparge', this water is stored in a separate tank from the wort, and recycled as the first water of the next cycle. Some distillers also use a fourth water, recycled as the second water.

Below

A mash tun at Cardhu. Mashing is a crucial stage in the production of malt whisky and demands rigorous temperature control.

Mashing can take from four to ten hours, with some distillers believing 'the slower the better.'

Mash tuns are generally stainless steel, although Caol Ila and Edradour are among the traditionalists using cast iron. Edradour's dates from the early 1900s, and there is no desire to change it in case the flavour profile is affected.

The residue grist, referred to as 'spent grain' or 'draff', is sold while still wet (with a moisture level of 75–80 per cent), and used as cattle feed.

WASHBACKS

Wort is cooled prior to fermentation within the wort cooler, which operates by running cold water on the other side of metal plates. Edradour's traditional Open Works Cooler (also known as a Mortons Refridgerator), is still in service. Using the same principle, it comprises a large open tray with wort flowing over a series of copper pipes spanning the length of the tray. Cold water is conducted through the pipes, and wort entering the cooler at 64°C exits three minutes later at 20°C.

The cooled wort is then conducted to a washback, a large vessel in which it is fermented by adding yeast. Washbacks are constructed either of wood or stainless steel, with each entailing different characteristics.

Wooden washbacks, either larch or pine, are harder to clean and require up to two hose downs

Above
Wooden
washbacks at
Lagavulin in the
past. At some
distilleries these
were cleaned by
men who
climbed inside
the tub and
scoured them
with a 'besom' of
birch or twigs.

followed by steam-cleaning. A single hose down is generally sufficient for a stainless steel washback. However, the question of cleaning is not simply a practical one. Wooden washbacks entail a higher level of bacterial presence than stainless steel, which may sound alarming but this is essentially lactic acid, as found in live yogurt. Moreover, some bacterial presence is considered a positive influence on the resulting flavour profile. However, lactic acid bacteria present in the washback also compete against the yeast for the fermentable sugars, converting them into lactic acid rather than the desirable ethanol, and resulting in a lower alcohol yield.

Some distillers believe wooden washbacks

control the temperature better (an important factor during fermentation) on the basis that wood heats and cools more gradually than stainless steel. However, many are reluctant to change from wood to stainless steel (or vice versa), in case it alters the range of flavour compounds.

YEAST

Although wort possesses cereal characteristics, it only develops the flavour compounds evident in new make spirit through fermentation. As different types of yeast promote varying flavour compounds, choosing which type(s) to use is a crucial decision.

Distiller's yeast and brewer's yeast are the two principal types used, with various strains of each

Below

Washbacks were originally made of Douglas fir or larch, but stainless steel has long been the norm as it is easier to clean.

Above
The types and
quantities of
yeast used
are carefully
chosen and
calculated as
this influences
the flavour of
the resulting
whisky.

available. The two principal strains of distiller's yeast used are Quest M and Mauri Pinnacle, with so-called 'fast acting' and 'slow acting' strains available of each type. Both behave as their names suggest, with some distillers combining the two strains to ensure more sustained action during fermentation.

Brewer's yeast has a different genetic profile to distiller's yeast, and varies further according to the brewery from which it is sourced. In some instances, only distiller's yeast is used, which is able to ferment slightly longer chain sugars than brewer's yeast, and therefore provide the highest alcohol yield. Meanwhile, some distillers believe that adding brewer's yeast makes no difference.

Distillers who combine both types of yeast say it promotes a fuller fermentation and an additional flavour profile. At Bowmore, for example, the primary floral aromas of lavendar and lilac are attributed to a combined use of distiller's and brewer's yeast.

Some distillers even take a 'multi-option', combining for instance two strains of distiller's yeast with two strains of brewer's yeast, on the basis that a more complex yeast formula results in a more complex range of flavours.

Yeast is delivered to the distillery in a 'pressed', also known as 'caked', format, with the yeast drained of liquid and pressed into a cake. It has a shelf life of around one to two weeks, when stored on a refridgerated shelf at an optimum temperature of 2–4°C, and is reconstituted with cold water before being added to the wort.

An alternative is dried yeast, which is used by a minority of distillers for practical reasons. An isolated location may prevent regular deliveries of fresh yeast, particularly during heavy snowfalls. Dried yeast also keeps for up to a year and does not require refridgeration. All it requires to be activated is blending with warm water.

Two formulas are used to calculate the amount of yeast required for each washback (which vary greatly in size), and relate either to the total litres of wort, or the original tonnage of malt. At some distilleries between 12kg and 14kg of yeast are used per ton of barley, while the size of the washback means that at one distillery 125kg is added to 42,000 litres of wort, with another adding 250kg to 66,500 litres.

Temperature and timing are crucial considerations during fermentation. As the temperature rises during fermentation, and as yeast expires at around 34°C, all the fermentable sugars within the wort need to be converted into alcohol by that stage, (yeast also expires once all the sugars are fermented).

Consequently, distillers decide on a pitching

temperature at which to begin fermentation. This is established by cooling the wort to that temperature, and so ensuring that fermentation is completed before the cut-off point for yeast. This typically means reaching a peak of 30–32°C during fermentation, to include a safety margin.

The pitching temperature also determines the rate and length of fermentation, which has an important influence on the flavour profile formed by the yeast. A lower pitching temperature, of around 16–19°C, initiates a slower start and rate of fermentation, whereas 20–22°C sees the process begin and conclude more rapidly.

The slower the better is the opinion of many distillers, with 36 hours generally quoted as the minimum, although fermentation often ranges from 45–100 hours. A slower fermentation is said to promote spicier, fruitier notes although, if too slow it can yield a grainy or solventy element. Too rapid a fermentation can add nuttiness.

As the pitching temperature is often the only form of heat control, it may be lowered by a few degrees on a hot day. However, some distilleries also use cooling jackets, through which cold water is conducted, around the washbacks.

Once yeast is added to the wort it technically becomes wash, although this term is generally applied to the liquid once it has fermented. Essentially a form of crude beer, containing yeast cells and the residue of malted barley, the wash has an alcoholic strength of around 7–8 per cent.

DISTILLING

The wash is distilled twice in copper pot stills, with copper reacting against volatile sulphurous compounds, and effectively 'cleaning' the spirit. Otherwise flavour compounds can be masked or even overwhelmed. Copper is also more effective than stainless steel in 'fixing' the characteristics of the new make spirit.

The pot still is the most traditional method of distillation. Effectively a circular kettle, the design is virtually unchanged since the Dutch invented this process in the 16th century. Distillation is based on the principle that alcohol boils at a lower temperature than water. Heating a fermented liquid within an enclosed container, drawing off the alcoholic vapours, then cooling and

Above

The still room at Caol Ila with the Paps of Jura mountains in the background.

45

condensing these vapours, yields an alcoholic spirit.

The first distillation is undertaken using a wash still. By heating the wash to the point when the alcohol vapourises, the vapours are driven up the still and along the neck, through the lye pipe (or lyne arm), and into the condenser, where the vapours condense back into a liquid form. This yields a distillate known as 'low wines', with a strength of around 20–25 per cent abv.

The first distillation effectively shapes the character of the new make spirit, which is then refined by a second distillation in a separate spirit still. This passes through another condenser, and is collected in the spirit receiver. As the second distillation entails a smaller amount of liquid, spirit stills generally have a smaller capacity than wash stills.

The second distillation run entails three phases: the foreshots (or heads), the spirit cut, and the feints (or tails). The foreshots and feints, being the initial and concluding stages of the distillation run, are of an unsuitable quality and alcoholic strength, which declines as the distillation run continues. Foreshots and feints are collected to be redistilled with the next batch of low wines.

Only the spirit cut is collected as new make spirit, with the parameters based on alcoholic strength, which incorporates quality control. Most distillers collect the spirit cut at an average of 70 per cent abv, which means starting to collect

Opposite
The stills
at Aberlour.

46

spirit from around 73–75 per cent abv, down to around 68–64.5 per cent abv. In terms of the flavour profile, a guideline is that pungent, fruity esters are more evident in spirit collected at 72–68 per cent abv, while a spirit cut that extends to around 58 per cent abv includes heavier, oilier, fatty acids.

The spirit cut represents around 20 per cent of the total distillation run. However, some distillers take a smaller spirit cut, at 16–17 per cent of the total, claiming that this yields more consistent quality and more concentrated spirit. However, this also entails more recycling and energy to run the still.

HEATING THE STILL

The flavour profile of the new make spirit is also influenced by the rate of distillation, which depends on the temperature to which the still is heated. Increasing the heat means a faster rate of distillation, and a higher proportion of heavier flavour compounds vapourising from the wash. A lower temperature and gentler rate of distillation promotes lighter characteristics, and, according to some distillers, a finer quality spirit. The spirit cut can be collected as slowly as around nine litres per minute, compared to a peak of around 20 litres a minute.

How to heat the still is another element of the debate. The traditional method of direct

Opposite
Longmorn's stills are unusual in being fired by direct heat; most stills are fitted with steam-heated coils.

heating, using a coal fire or gas flame, was largely replaced in the 1960s–70s by using steam conducted through pipes within the boil pot (base), of the still.

Steam coils are generally considered to provide the best heat control and distribution within the still. Adjusting the temperature by shutting off the steam is much simpler than controlling a coal fire. Better heat control also avoids burning or caramelising the wash, which is a potential threat with direct heat. However, some exponents of direct heating cite the positive aspect of a slight charring effect, which can carry over into the resulting whisky.

Glenfiddich is unusual in using gas and coal-fired stills. A series of concentric gas rings under each still ensures a uniform temperature, (copper also transmits heat very quickly). Meanwhile, air is 'blasted' into the coal fire, ensuring uniform heat, with extra fuel added automatically to maintain the appropriate temperature.

STILL DESIGN

As the flavour profile of new make spirit is also influenced by the size and shape of the stills, distilleries have their own design variations, however subtle.

A taller, narrower still promotes lighter, more delicate notes, as the taller the still the greater the degree of 'reflux'. This is because heavier, denser, oilier flavour compounds have a higher boiling point than lighter flavour compounds. As they rise up the still, the temperature becomes relatively cooler, which means that they condense back into liquid and return to the boil pot of the still.

Glenmorangie's stills are an ultimate in the industry, extending 16 feet, 10 1/4 inches (5.13 meters), a height that dates from 1880. This higher degree of reflux promotes a light, floral, fragrant new make spirit with a sweet edge.

The degree of reflux can also be increased by including a boil bowl, an additional bulbous section above the boil pot and below the neck.

Below
Glenmorangie – the tallest stills in the industry.

When vapours carrying heavier flavour compounds reach the boil bowl, they expand into this larger and relatively cooler area, where they start condensing and return to the boil pot.

A shorter, onion-shaped still with a wider neck means less temperature variation. This promotes the progress of heavier flavour compounds into the condenser, yielding fuller-bodied, denser spirit with a creamier, earthier, oilier texture. Similarly, a still with a shorter neck promotes a balance of oilier flavours reaching the condenser.

The angle of the lye pipe is another important influence. A lye pipe conducts the vapours from the neck of the still to the condenser. If it extends at an incline, it encourages a greater level of condensation, driving heavier flavour compounds back into the still. Alternatively, a descending lye pipe encourages a wider and heavier range to reach the condenser. Similarly, a shorter lye pipe means less reflux, while a longer pipe extends the degree of contact with copper.

CONDENSING THE VAPOURS

Whether to use a worm or a 'shell and tube' condenser is another consideration (condensation begins as soon as the vapours enter either). Needless to say, exponents of each method promote its superiority over the alternative.

Most distilleries use a condenser, comprising

numerous copper pipes which the vapours enter, with cold water conducted on the other side of the pipes. By providing a greater surface area than a typical worm, the contact between the spirit and copper is increased, helping to strip out sulphurous compounds.

A worm is the more historic method, being a coiled copper pipe of decreasing diameter, set in a worm tub through which cold water circulates. While worms can offer less surface area contact with copper, this does not neccessarily result in a higher level of sulphurous, meaty flavour compounds. The challenge for the distiller is controlling the level of these characteristics to achieve a complex whisky. This can be achieved by a slower fermentation (reducing the level of sulphurous compounds within the wash), as well as controlling the rate of distillation, with the size and shape of the still also influential. Moreover, worms can be incredibly long, which obviously extends the degree of contact with copper.

Worm tubs, constructed of cast iron or wood such as larch, are an *al fresco* feature, with the lye pipe extending through the wall of the still house, reaching the worm and worm tub which adjoin the external wall, so benefitting from the ambient temperature.

The residue of the first distillation run, known as 'pot ale', is a thick liquid including spent yeast cells, with a strength of less than one per cent abv, which is bought by farmers as a form of fertiliser. Boiling this residue produces pot ale syrup, with the reduced volume making it more economical to transport. Spent lees, the residue of the second distillation, is processed through the distillery's own water purification plant.

NEW MAKE SPIRIT

The quality of the new make spirit is crucial, as aging may refine it but cannot elevate the quality. The master distiller assesses new make spirit on the level of esters (which provide fragrant fruitiness), phenols (peat, smokiness, medicinal

Below
A master distiller assessing new make spirit.

notes) and feintiness (cereal, leather, tobacco, beeswax), as appropriate to the house style.

Strathisla new make spirit, for example, yields mellow barley, fruity notes. The Macallan is lightly perfumed, floral with a hint of barley, linseed oil, and apple, pear drops. Highland Park is apple sweet with a certain smokiness, while Bowmore has sweet malty notes with fruity, pear characteristics.

AGING

Like all spirits, malt whisky was originally drunk unaged, fresh from the still. The benefits of aging were discovered when spirits stored and transported in barrels were found to arrive with a mellower, rounder flavour, particularly if a long sea crossing was involved.

Malt whisky must be aged in Scotland for a minimum of three years, in oak casks with a maximum capacity of 700 litres. While the stipulations are exact, the process of maturation is not an exact science as it depends on various factors beyond the character of the new make spirit, including the conditions under which the spirit is aged and the type of barrel.

While some distilleries may only use barrels that previously aged either Sherry or Bourbon for certain brands, many utilise both types. Each type of barrel offers varying characteristics that influence the flavour profile imparted to the spirit.

Exactly how influential the oak is depends on whom you ask, though a consensus is around 60 per cent (some even say 70 per cent), of the malt's eventual flavour profile. On Islay, the high level of peating means the barrel may account for around 40 per cent. In addition to refining the malt, the intention is for the whisky to retain the distillery's house style.

Oak not only passes on various beneficial characteristics, but also removes undesirable, harsher elements from the spirit. Being permeable, oak allows air to pass through the barrel, mellowing the whisky and enhancing the flavour. The nature of the air can also be influential, with sea air detectable as sea spray notes, which can also promote citrus characteristics in some malts aged on the coast.

Three sizes of cask are generally used for maturation. A barrel (with a capacity of 180–200 litres) exerts the greatest influence on the spirit, due to a larger surface area contact with the wood in relation to the volume of whisky. This also initiates a faster rate of maturity. Similarly, a hogshead (250–305 litres) imparts a greater influence and matures spirit more rapidly than a butt (500 litres). Which size is the most appropriate depends on the degree of oak influence desired, with some distillers, for example, only using butts.

How often a barrel has been used or filled with malt whisky is another consideration. The usual

Right
The warehouse at The Macallan distillery.

life-cycle is up to three or four fills, which can mean 50 years active service. This practice accounts for the reference 'first fill', meaning a barrel filled with whisky for the first time. 'Second fill' refers to a barrel filled with whisky for the second time, and so on.

Each time a barrel is used, the degree to which it influences the spirit is diminished. If a first fill barrel is said to contribute 100 per cent of its characteristics, this declines to around 60 per cent during its second fill, 35 per cent in the third, and 5–10 per cent in the fourth fill. In terms of the maturation rate, this means the same whisky could mature within seven or eight years in a first fill barrel, 10–11 years in a second fill, and around 15 years in a third fill. However, the only way to monitor progress is for the master distiller to take samples. Similarly, as different barrels have varying life-cycles, the master distiller also monitors barrels based on the colour, and flavour, yielded to the spirit.

Distillers generally use a combination of various fills, depending on the degree of oak influence desired; which might mean only first and second fill, or all four fills. A lighter, unpeated malt for example, may principally be aged in second fill barrels, ensuring the wood influence isn't overpowering.

Each time a barrel was filled it traditionally received a colour coding and numerical reference painted on the head or end. Using less colourful but more efficient bar codes has reduced the time needed for stocktaking from up to a couple of months to a couple of days.

Barrels are invariably filled with new make spirit at a strength of 63.5 per cent abv. (If the spirit comes off the still at a higher strength, it is reduced by adding water.) This strength is considered a perfect balance between the subsequent rate of maturation and the amount of casks required to mature it.

Although malt whisky matures more rapidly at a lower alcoholic strength, this would also mean a greater volume of whisky as larger amounts of water would be added. More casks and a larger area in which to age them would therefore be required – a serious financial consideration. Fewer casks are needed for malts barrelled at a higher strength, but this subsequently entails longer maturation, and many distillers believe malt whisky does not age as well at a higher strength. Some malts are barrelled at 68.5 per cent abv, in order to acquire a greater degree of wood characteristics, and are subsequently used for blending.

Filling the casks is a straightforward process at most distilleries, although there are exceptions. Edradour traditionally used three copper jugs (at five, four and one gallon capacity, respectively), to lower the strength of new make spirit from around 70 per cent abv to 63.5 per cent abv. However, in 1995 the distillery took a big step forward, introducing the current method of a hose and water meter. Despite such progress, this still entails a lot of work as 14 casks (each with a 250 litre capacity), are filled each week.

BOURBON BARRELS

Barrels used to age Bourbon are made from new white American oak, usually harvested in Iowa, Illinois, Missouri and Arkansas. The barrels are charred on the inside by applying a flame, with Bourbon distillers stipulating the degree of charring using a scale of 1–4. A number one char resembles burnt toast, with a number four popularly termed an alligator char, as the cracked, segmented surface resembles alligator hide.

The surface level of char is effectively pure carbon, typically two mm deep, with heavy charring reaching four mm. An underlying 2–3 mm is also altered by the heat during charring, resulting in partially caramelised wood sugar, and this layer is instrumental in releasing flavour compounds such as vanilla. The majority of the stave (up to 20 mm), remains unaffected by charring and is a minor influence.

By breaking up the surface of the oak, charring enables the spirit to penetrate the wood more readily. This in turn accelerates the 'release' of flavour compounds in the underlying layer, with a particular flourish during the first few years of the first fill. Charring also acts as a charcoal filter, helping to remove undesirable compounds, which accelerates the aging process. The residue level of Bourbon within the staves of a barrel can be around 75cl, but this is a minor influence compared to the oak, and only has some impact during the first fill.

The tradition of using charred barrels is popularly attributed to the Rev. Elijah Craig, possibly because he provides the most colourful anecdote. A preacher and entrepreneur based in Georgetown, Kentucky, he was also a distiller, which may reflect his Scottish ancestry. On what seemed like an ordinary day in 1789, a cooper accidentally scorched some staves being made up

Left
Charring barrels breaks up the surface of the oak, promoting a greater interaction between the spirit and wood.

into a barrel. They were still used anyway, perhaps by mistake or simply for economy. Whiskey aged in this barrel was found to be smoother and rounder, not to mention a more attractive colour. This 'radical' whiskey soon became known as 'Bourbon', after the county in which various distillers were based.

Charring may also stem from barrels originally being a multi-purpose means of storage. Barrels previously holding salted fish, pickled herrings or cabbage, for instance, may have been used to mature whiskey. In order to remove every trace of the barrel's former occupant, the interior was routinely charred. Another possibility is that charring evolved from the traditional practice of burning straw inside a barrel in order to sterilise it.

It was also a Scotsman working in the American whiskey business, Jim Crow, who gets the credit for promoting the use of charred barrels. He is thought to be the first distiller to mature his entire consignment of Bourbon in charred barrels during the 1820s.

Regulations state that Bourbon distillers can only use barrels once, with a minimum aging period of two years. This ensures a ready supply of barrels for resale to Scotch whisky distillers. Canadian whisky, rum and tequila are among other spirits also aged in Bourbon barrels.

Right
Assembling the
casks in
a Speyside
cooperage.

Malt whisky distillers began using Bourbon barrels in far greater quantities during the Spanish civil war in 1936–9, and World War II, when

Sherry casks were obviously harder to source. Ocassionally Bourbon barrels are dismantled in Kentucky and shipped as 'shooks' (staves). This reduces transport costs, but must be balanced against an invoice from a cooper reassembling the barrels in Scotland. Sometimes staves are reassembled into a different sized cask (boosted by extra staves), in which case they are given the prefix 'dump' or 'remake'.

Some distillers are experimenting with 'spent' Bourbon barrels, stripping the char and recharring, to see whether it provides a new lease of life. Others are assessing whether charring individual staves (prior to being fashioned into a barrel), provides any different influences to charring a completed barrel.

SHERRY CASKS

The amount of Sherry casks used to mature malt whisky is a fraction compared to Bourbon barrels, with an estimated 15,000 Sherry casks acquired each year by the Scotch whisky industry, compared to around 600–800,000 Bourbon barrels.

The tradition of using Sherry casks stems entirely from practicality. Sherry was originally shipped to the UK in casks, principally to the ports of Bristol and Leith, and then bottled locally. As the UK was a major Sherry market there was an abundance of empty casks to be had.

However, during the 1980s, Sherry houses moved to bottling at source in Jerez. As fewer new casks were needed, production levels and availability naturally decreased.

Acquiring Sherry barrels is now a more involved and more expensive process, with a sherry butt currently around £400, (compared to around £90 for two Bourbon barrels totalling the same capacity). Sherry houses also take a fee from distillers for seasoning the casks with their Sherry, which they also retain and subsequently commercialise. Seasoning is vital to flush out undesirable elements, such as the overt spiciness characteristic of all virgin oak.

A first fill Sherry barrel obviously passes on a considerable influence. Traditionally, much of this influence was attributed to the residue amount of Sherry 'drunk in' by the staves, which could mean up to 10 litres in a 500 litre cask. However, recent research concludes that the oak, not the Sherry, is the principal benefactor. The second fill sees the cask's influence diminish by about 50–75 per cent, and its influence is

Below

The Balvenie DoubleWood is matured first in Bourbon oak and then in Sherry oak.

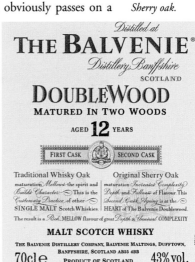

65

Right
Sherry barrels
stacked in the
traditional
manner.

minimal by the third fill. The fill used reflects the house style, with a first fill Sherry barrel considered too rich and overpowering for some malts. In this case, Sherry barrels may be further seasoned by aging malt whisky for about 12 years (with this malt reserved for blending), and only whisky from the second fill of such a barrel would be bottled as a single malt.

As The Macallan only uses Sherry barrels, the company accounts for around 65 per cent of the Sherry barrels used by the Scotch whisky industry. This represents a grand total of around 20,000 casks continually being matured on behalf of the company in Spain. Not surprisingly, The Macallan has specific requirements for the barrels, which are assembled using oak from 150-year-old trees, cultivated in Galicia, and subsequently air-dried for at least two years in Andalucia to a moisture level of 14 per cent. Air-drying is preferable to kiln-drying (which is applied to some types of oak), as this slower process entails some bacterial presence which in turn promotes the tannins within the wood.

Casks are seasoned by initially filling them with palomino must (the juice pressed from palomino grapes, from which Sherry is produced). This ferments inside the barrel and can take 10–15 days or longer. No yeast is added as fermentation occurs naturally due to the yeasts present in the grape skins. Once drained of fermented wine, after a season of perhaps several months, barrels are filled with dry Oloroso Sherry, at a strength of 17.5 per cent abv. This remains in the barrel for two to three years before being emptied. Whether barrels that have held different styles of Sherry subsequently pass on these differentials to malt whisky is another consideration. Trials conducted by The Macallan concluded that butts previously holding various styles of Sherry, ranging from dry Fino to sweet Oloroso, did not impart significant flavour differences to malt aged for 18 years. However, when barrels that held various styles of Sherry are used for 'finishing' (see page 81) the differences are more readily apparent.

THE DIFFERENCES IN USING BOURBON AND SHERRY CASKS

Whether a barrel previously contained Bourbon or Sherry is not as significant as the type of oak it was made from. An initial consideration is that Spanish and American oak are different species, although some Sherry casks are also made from American oak.

Spanish oak (quercus robur), is harvested from 60–150-year-old trees, and has a looser, more open and porous grain than American oak, enabling the spirit to penetrate the oak more readily. It also has a far greater level of tannins than American oak, which add astringency, balance and structure. American oak (quercus alba), is harvested from 40–100-year-old trees, and has a straighter, tighter grain.

While Bourbon casks are charred on the inside, Sherry casks are only lightly toasted, although this also helps open up the surface layer. As the Solera method used to age Sherry can entail stacking barrels several high on top of each other, staves have to be strong, at around 38mm thick compared to Bourbon barrels at around 25mm. Thicker staves may imply a greater level of flavour compounds available to the spirit. However, any benefits are only passed on where the spirit makes contact with the oak, and even if the spirit penetrates beyond the toasted layer, the influence is minimal.

An immediate distinction between the influence of these two types of oak is the colour imparted to the spirit. Sherry casks contribute an orangey, amber, mahogany hue, compared to the lighter, golden, straw tint from Bourbon barrels. The flavours imparted also vary. Sherry barrels yield rich fruit, fruit cake, raisin, resin, fortified wine, almond and walnut notes, with a rich, dry sweetness. Bourbon barrels pass on vanilla, honey,

Below
The Aberlour range of malts includes various maturation influences, as well as a non chill-filtered style.

a range of fruit flavours, almond, hazlenut, coconut, and spicy notes such as cinnamon and ginger, with a lighter, drier sweetness.

OTHER TYPES OF BARRELS

Oak barrels in which other spirits and styles of fortified wine have been matured provide further options. Springbank Distillery, for example, uses Port barrels. After several years aging, the spirit shows the colour and some characteristics of Ruby Port, *en route* to a total maturation period of 10–12 years. Springbank is also using Rum barrels (generally Demerara rum), which contribute a spicy top note and a depth of sweetness and balance. The distillery previously offered a limited edition bottling of malt matured

Right
The Balvenie
PortWood is
initially aged in
Bourbon oak
and then
put into
Portuguese oak
casks used to age
30-year-old port.

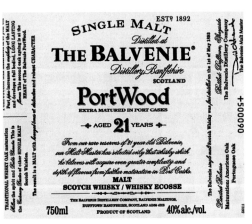

in Rum barrels and is experimenting with Bordeaux barrels, previously used to mature red wine. Various types of barrels are also used for finishing (see page 81).

AGING

Financing stocks of maturing whisky is obviously a significant investment for a distillery. Moreover, the lengthy maturation periods involved also entail predicting future demand and laying down sufficient stock. The amount of mature and maturing whisky in Scotland currently represents about ten years of projected future sales.

The conditions under which whisky is matured also influence the rate of maturity and flavour profile. Cool, humid and stable temperatures are ideal, with greater humidity promoting a gentler maturation. Seasonal effects on the spirit, known as a 'cycle,' see the liquid gently 'expand' during warmer temperatures and penetrate the oak, while cooler weather sees it 'contract'. The intensity of the cycle obviously varies among distilleries, though by penetrating the oak more deeply, the level of flavour compounds gained by the spirit is correspondingly higher.

While the temperature inside a warehouse obviously reflects the local climate, (with Islay for example, having a temperate climate throughout the year), another factor is that the volume of whisky within a warehouse acts as an 'insulator'.

Consequently, a vast temperature differential outside the warehouse is required to affect the interior. A warehouse in Speyside, for example, where the external temperature may vary from -25°C to 25°C in winter and summer, sees an annual range of between 4–12°C respectively within the warehouse.

Temperature also affects the rate of evaporation, which increases as the temperature rises. Evaporation accounts for about 2–2.5 per cent of the contents of a barrel per annum, with the vapours rising to the heavens referred to as the 'angels' share'. As evaporation includes water and alcohol, there is a gradual decline in the alcoholic strength and concentration of the spirit. The evaporation rate then begins to slow down as alcoholic strength declines. This means a malt barrelled at 63.5 per cent abv may reach 58 per cent abv after 12 years, 56 per cent abv after 18 years, 54–55 per cent abv after 25 years, and 46–50 per cent abv after 50 years.

TYPES OF WAREHOUSES

Two principal types of warehouse are used to age malt whisky: traditional (also known as dunnage), and racked (also known as commercial). An aging warehouse typically includes malts from across a range of ages. This ensures that in the case of a fire, all the malt whisky of a particular year is not lost, and various

ages remain available to the master distiller from other warehouses.

A traditional warehouse is regarded as five star, deluxe accommodation for malts. This means a brick or stone building with thick walls and a low slate roof. An earthern floor helps keep the warehouse humid, and encourages greater penetration of air into the barrels. A traditional warehouse also has the best circulation of air, keeping average temperatures warmer and more stable.

However, a traditional warehouse is less economical to operate than a racked warehouse,

Above
Stacked barrels in a traditional warehouse.

particularly if the malts are intended for blending rather than bottling as single malts. Barrels can only be stacked a maximum of three high, resting on top of each other – more than this and the weight bearing down on underlying barrels would be too much – which means far fewer barrels can be stored than in a racked warehouse. Another consideration is that fork lift trucks can only operate in some traditional warehouses, which means many barrels have to be moved manually.

Racked warehouses, dating from the 1960s, are used to age single malts and malts for blending. Built of brick, cement blocks or a steel clad structure, they feature tall racks with galvanised steel rails on which the barrels rest, stacked up to eight or even 12 barrels high. This means barrels at the top of the warehouse experience slightly different conditions to those at the bottom, though any differences are balanced by marrying (see page 76). Some racked warehouses limit the extent of concrete to pathways between racks, with earthern sections under the racks. This 'traditional' element helps to reduce the temperature range between the top and bottom of the warehouse. Needless to say, fork lift trucks can easily negotiate racked warehouses.

Palletised warehouses, a 1980s concept, are generally the preserve of grain whisky, though they may also be used to age malt. Usually built of brick with a concrete floor, this type of warehouse is named after the manner in which

Right

A palletised warehouse is essentially used for grain whisky, though may also include some malt whisky. The evaporation rate is higher than in a racked warehouse but these warehouses are cheaper to run.

barrels are stored, standing upright on a pallete, rather than horizontal as in a traditional or racked warehouse.

As each pallete typically holds six barrels, a warehouse stacked six or seven palletes high represents a maximum use of space. The cylindrical shape of Bourbon barrels is more suited to this approach than the more curvaceous Sherry barrels. However, stacking palletes so close together results in less air flow, a wider range of temperatures than a racked warehouse, and a slightly higher rate of evaporation. The compensating factor is that palletised warehouses are the least expensive to run.

MARRYING

Once a malt whisky is pronounced mature, it undergoes a very important ceremony: the marriage. This consists of individual casks being combined in a large vessel known as a marrying vat, to integrate them thoroughly prior to bottling. While two months is often considered the minimum marrying period, the schedule varies among distilleries. Younger whiskies, of eight years or less, require a longer marrying period, which entails a general 'smoothing' effect, (a quality already inherent in longer aged malts).

Various forms of 'marriage ceremonies' are utilised. The malts may be combined for a short period within a wood or stainless steel marrying vat prior to bottling, or the whisky may be decanted back into casks from the marrying vat for a further period, before being revatted to prevent any possible variations.

Another option involves using a marrying vat that continually retains a residual amount of malt from an existing marriage. For example, a single malt may involve a 'recipe' of whiskies that have undergone a range of maturation influences, including first, second and third fill Sherry and Bourbon casks. Around 25–30,000 litres of malt whisky from these various barrels may be emptied into a vat with a 100,000 litre capacity, which already holds 50,000 litres of an existing marriage. The vat features a 'rouser' that gently circulates like a propellor for thorough integration. A batch of spirit is subsequently drawn from the base of the marrying vat, which retains a minimum of 50,000 litres.

Prior to bottling, whisky is reduced to bottling strength by adding water, with 40 per cent abv being the minimum strength. When whisky is diluted with water it has the significant effect of separating the alcohol and existing water. A resting period (often around 24 hours), is then required to achieve re-integration.

FILTRATION

Prior to bottling, the great majority of Scotch whisky is chill-filtered. This practice became standard during the 1960s and ensures that whisky bottled at below 46 per cent abv retains its clarity. Without chill-filtering, whisky below this strength would have a cloudy haze either when diluted with water, or when subjected to lower temperatures, such as adding ice. Similarly, whisky stored at a low temperature would throw a haze in the bottle.

However, what is gained in terms of clarity through chill-filtering may also entail a reduction in mouthfeel and certain flavour compounds, which can compromise an element of the depth, complexity and finish.

The lower the temperature at which whisky is chill-filtered, the greater the reduction of certain compounds. Chill-filtering at 4°C stabilises the whisky, at the loss of some compounds that can heighten mouthfeel. A temperature of -4°C entails loosing more mouthfeel and some flavour compounds. However, if the house style is a lighter whisky, this may not necessarily be a loss.

STYLES OF WHISKY

An initial guide to the varying characteristics of malt whisky reflects the location of the distillery, within designated regions.

Lowland malts are renowned as the lightest, sweetest, most delicately flavoured with fruity, floral, honeyed notes.

Highland malts span the largest range of

characteristics, reflecting the region's geographical extent and diversity, although balanced complexity is a key feature. Malts range from drier, peatier styles, through spicier, heathery, honeyed examples, to fruitier characteristics bearing apple, pear, citrus, raisin and other dried fruit notes.

Speyside lies within the Highland region but its specific climatic conditions endow malts with distinct characteristics. In fact, Speyside is considered to produce some of the most sophisticated malts, which explains why around half the total number of Scotch whisky distilleries are located there. Speyside malts deliver distinguished, ripe fruit and floral notes, together with great structure, complexity and elegance.

Campbeltown malts, from Campbeltown in the Mull of Kintyre, feature peated malts with marine, sea air characteristics. Islay malts,

Left

Islay malts are renowned for a distinctive style, spanning robust, peaty, smokey, notes, supported by a range of vanilla, dried fruit and citrus notes, that add up to an intriguing complex total.

produced by several distilleries on the island of Islay, are considered to be the most robust and pungent. However, they also offer subtlety and finesse, with a characteristic range of smokey, peaty, medicinal, iodine notes, not to mention seaweed, sea air and citrus overtones.

MALT WHISKY TERMINOLOGY

Beyond Single Malt (the product of one distillery), and Vatted Malts (a marriage of malts from more than one distillery), the range continues to grow with ever-more rarified styles.

Single Barrel malt whisky bottled from a single barrel appeals to connoisseurs, as even two neighbouring barrels in a warehouse, filled with

Right
Single barrel malt – even two neighbouring barrels in a warehouse, filled with the same new make spirit and aged for the same period are never identical.

SINGLE MALT
Distilled at
THE BALVENIE®
Distillery, Banffshire
SCOTLAND
SINGLE BARREL
MALT SCOTCH WHISKY
from a single barrel
AGED **15** YEARS

the same new make spirit and aged for the same period, are never identical.

Cask Strength malt whisky, bottled at the alcoholic strength it reaches on maturity within the cask, has been driven by growing specialist interest since the mid-1990s. As this style includes malts which are not chill-filtered, it has an additional appeal. Alcoholic strengths can vary from around 43–65 per cent abv.

Vintage malt whisky has also emerged more significantly since the mid-1990s, and is a specialty of such distilleries as The Glenlivet. As the product of a single year, there can be annual variations in the new make spirit, which may reflect factors such as changing from one barley variety to another. However, the choice of barrels and aging conditions essentially account for variations, which may not always be dramatic but there is a discernible individuality. Vintage malt is a limited edition, intensifying the appeal for connoisseurs, with a malt such as The Balvenie 1967 comprising a total release of 700 bottles worldwide.

Special finishes have proved to be a dynamic sector since being pioneered by Glenmorangie in 1994. A finish (a 'secondary' maturation period in a specific type of barrel), contributes a garnish of top notes, which provides an added dimension of character and flavour, enhancing the character of the malt. This technique principally utilises barrels previously used to age fortified wine,

Above
Vintage malt has become increasingly popular since the mid 1990s.

Above Glenmorangie pioneered special finishes which enhance the character and the flavour of the malt.

including Sherry, Port and Madeira, which offer a richness and sweetness that integrates successfully with malt.

The Glenmorangie Wood Finish range sees malt whiskies initially matured in Bourbon casks for at least 10 years, then 'finished' in casks previously containing either Ruby Port, Malmsey Madeira or Fino Sherry. A subsequent introduction is a Malaga wood finish, using casks that previously held this rare sweet wine from the Malaga region of Spain.

The Distiller's Edition of the Classic Malts Collection offers a specific choice of finish in various styles of Sherry casks, with Glenkinchie finished in Amontillado, Dalwhinnie in Oloroso, Oban in Montilla Fino, Talisker in Amoroso (a sweetened style of Oloroso), and Lagavulin in Pedro-Ximenez casks.

The duration of a finish can vary, with Glenmorangie applying an 18 month to two year finishing period, which compares to nine months in Oloroso Sherry casks for The Balvenie 12-year-old Double Wood.

Oak barrels previously used to mature various styles of wine are also utilised for finishing. Following a main maturation period in Bourbon barrels, Glen Moray uses white wine barrels previously used to age either Chardonnay or Chenin Blanc. Chardonnay oak for instance, adds freshness, zesty grapefruit and grapeyness, along with American soda, ice cream notes.

Barrels previously holding red wine also provide opportunities. Glenmorangie has released a 1975 vintage with a Cote de Nuits Burgundy cask finish, yielding balanced sweetness, fruit and deep vinous notes. Bordeaux casks, previously used to age a classic red Bordeaux blend, provide a two year finishing period for Bowmore Dusk Bordeaux Wine Casked, after at least 12 years maturation in Bourbon and Sherry casks. This adds an abundance of red fruit notes, including redcurrants, wild cherries, rosehip syrup, raspberries and damsons, with a creamy 'sherbert fizz'

Below
French oak barrels add further spice and depth to the malt.

emerging mid-palate.

Among distillers using casks that previously held spirits, Gordon & MacPhail's Private Collection includes a Cognac wood finish, with one version using a Speyside malt distilled at Imperial, and another using an Islay malt produced at Caol Ila. A two year Calvados finish is also available in two versions, using the same malts as the Cognac finish.

To add another dimension, New American and French oak barrels can also be used for finishing, adding further spice and depth. The Glenlivet American Oak Finish uses new white American oak barrels, with new Limousin oak used for The Glenlivet French Oak Finish. The oak's origin within France is also important. Oak from the Troncais forest is renowned for its soft, fine grain, which contributes smooth tannins and a more pronounced vanilla flavour than Limousin oak, which is medium-grained, even more porous, and renowned for contributing strength and balance.

The innovative Glenfiddich Solera Reserve also incorporates a new oak finish. This combines a high proportion of malts aged for 15 years in Bourbon and Sherry casks, together with malt aged for the same period exclusively in Sherry casks, as well as malt aged for 15 years in Bourbon

Above

The Glenfiddich Solera Reserve incorporates a new oak finish within a combination of malts aged in Bourbon and Sherry casks.

84

and Sherry casks which is subsequently finished for three to four months in new oak casks, (lending distinctive wood notes and a hint of coconut).

Whether organic malt whisky becomes an established style remains to be seen, with organic cognac, grappa, calvados, vodka and gin increasingly available, (not to mention organic tonic water, making it possible to have an OG&T). While organic is certainly a powerful marketing concept and ideal for such an innovative category as malt whisky, the degree to which organic status influences the flavour of the spirit is difficult to determine. Comparing organic to non-organic fruit and vegetables can readily demonstrate a difference in flavour, but there are numerous determining factors beyond the grain when producing an aged spirit.

The only way to prove the superiority of organic malt would be to produce spirit from neighbouring organic and non-organic fields, follow exactly the same production and maturation process, and compare the results several years later. This is unlikely to happen, and as already stated, even

Below

The first commercialised organic malt, Dà Mhìle, was produced at the Springbank distillery.

85

the same new make spirit aged in neighbouring barrels of the same provenance produces a slightly different result.

Opinions on the technical aspects of organic ingredients also vary. Some distillers believe there is no difference in the way organic ingredients behave during production. Others say organic grain ripens more slowly, offering higher starch levels and a higher alcohol yield per ton of grain. However, this must be balanced against a longer growing cycle, requiring larger investment.

The first commercialised organic malt whisky is Dà Mhìle (pronounced 'Daveelay'), Gaelic for 2000, and named after its release date. Produced by Springbank Distillery on behalf of an organic farmer, John Savage-Onstwedder, it was certified by the Soil Association Organic Standard. Ten tons of barley were distilled in 1992, yielding 15 barrels of malt whisky, which meant 4,000 bottles at cask strength, (around 60 per cent abv). John Savage-Onstwedder is continuing to develop organic malt whiskies.

THE ROLE OF MALTS IN BLENDED SCOTCH WHISKY

Despite the enormous growth of malts, the vast majority are combined with grain whisky to produce blended Scotch whisky, which accounts for around 95 per cent of total Scotch whisky sales. Grain whisky, distilled from maize or wheat, is essentially a lighter, more fragrant style. It is produced almost exclusively for blending but a limited amount is bottled as grain whisky.

Blending is a considerable art, often using between 15–50 individual whiskies of different ages, and from various distilleries, (even 'rival' distilleries readily trade malts among themselves). The objective is to combine whiskies that complement each other, producing a flavour that exceeds the sum of its individual components. Once blended, the whisky is returned to casks in order to 'marry,' allowing

Below
Various malts combine to create the character of Johnnie Walker Red Label.

the flavours to harmonise prior to bottling. The age statement on the bottle refers to the youngest whisky within the blend.

Blends can include a specific range of malts, with Black Bottle, for instance, featuring malts from seven Islay distilleries. Chivas Regal includes some of 'malt's greatest hits,' with the medicinal peaty, earthy, smokyness of Islay; the soft, fruity, vanilla notes of the Highlands; rich, rounded fruity notes from Speyside, and the drier, nutty character with an oakey hint courtesy of malt from the Strathisla distillery, to which grain whisky contributes a sweeter, vanilla element.

Tracing the role of a malt in various expressions of a Scotch whisky blend can be an interesting exercise. Johnnie Walker Red Label, for example, gains Sherry, malt flavours from Cardhu and other malts, with Talisker adding spice, some smokiness and smoothness. Meanwhile, Cardhu adds malt silkiness to Johnnie Walker Black Label.

THE IMPORTANCE OF THE NOSE

As the master distiller bases numerous decisions almost entirely on 'nosing' the aromas, this accounts for an alternative title: The Nose.
While a principal qualification for a master distiller is a superior olfactory sense, a good memory is also important, in order to recognise

Left
'Nosing' the whisky is the principal means of assessing its character and maturity.

the varying characteristics of the whiskies. As distilleries continue to extend their portfolios with ever-more styles, demands on the master distiller's nose continue to grow. A tasting panel can provide much needed back up, as of course can an extensive collection of notes.

As whiskies are sometimes also tasted, the master distiller's palate is trained alongside the nose. While the palate generally confirms what the nose has already ascertained, it can sometimes be a surprise, as nosing obviously cannot determine aspects such as the mouthfeel of an unfamiliar malt.

Above
Sometimes whisky is sampled straight from the cask in the warehouse, although this is rare due to the level of whisky fumes in the air.

A typical routine may mean nosing for about an hour daily, with 11am–12 noon the time when the senses are at their keenest. This can entail nosing up to 50–100 samples in batches of around eight at a time. Ten minute breaks inbetween batches prevent the nose from becoming saturated by alcohol, and samples are generally diluted to a strength of 20 per cent abv when nosing.

Strict conditions within the sampling room mean no after shave or perfume, and of course, no smoking. Even anyone present who has been smoking can affect the nosing. Sometimes nosing takes place in the aging warehouses, when checking samples drawn direct from the cask, although this isn't always ideal due to the level of whisky fumes in the air.

Computer technology increasingly helps the nose, as it can analyse samples for characteristics such as grain content, but it cannot begin to rival the nasal ability to assess samples. Technology also has its uses in keeping computerised records, but it is redundant in assessing the quality and life-cycle of a barrel.

Training a new recruit can entail around ten years of daily nosings, working alongside the master distiller. While future noses traditionally grew from among distillery employees, candidates now tend to apply with a science degree, and the length of training required means candidates are generally in their early 20s. An initial nosing test will determine potential, which is confirmed within the first two years of training.

GLEN SPEY
PURE MALT

SIX YEARS OLD

MADE ENTIRELY FROM
HOME GROWN BARLEY

BRAND DIRECTORY

All brands are 40 per cent abv
unless stated.

ABERLOUR

The distillery was built in 1879 by the site of St Drostan's Well, where an historic granite stone is linked to an ancient Druid community that occupied the valley of Aberlour. The name is Gaelic for 'mouth of the chattering burn.' Highland single malt.

TASTING NOTES – ABERLOUR

10 year old: elegant vanilla, honeyed aromas, with sherried, spicy hints. Smooth, rounded palate with sherried, honeyed, peaty sweetness and cinnamon, nutmeg notes. Fruity, malty, creamy finish. 43 per cent abv.

15-year-old Sherry Wood Finish: lightly smokey, toffee nose. Soft, permeating flavours with gently sherried honey and rounded vanilla. Rich finish releases more vanilla, honey and creamy lusciousness. 43 per cent abv.

18-year-old Sherry Matured: smokey, malty nose laced with sherry. Rich, rounded, fruity, honeyed palate with cinnamon and ginger. Smooth finish with oaky hints. 43 per cent abv.

21 year old: vanilla, almond and smokey oak aromas. Deeply malty palate, with honey, fruit, dark chocolate notes. Full finish with spicy hints. 43 per cent abv.

a'bunadh: sherried, honeyed nose with a waft of smoke and vanilla. Smooth, luscious palate with sherried, creamy, malty hints of cooked fruit and spice. Full-bodied though elegant finish with fruit cake, gingerbread and peaty hints. 59.6 per cent abv, non chill-filtered.

ARDBEG

Founded in 1815, it was reopened in 1997 when acquired by Glenmorangie plc. Islay single malt.

Above
The Ardbeg distillery.

TASTING NOTES – ARDBEG

10 year old: integrated smoke, peat and sea spray with overlying vanilla hints. Seamlessly integrated peat and citrus acidity, with sea spray at the edges. Rich, rounded finish with smokey, creamy malt. 46% abv, non chill-filtered.

17 year old: smokey vanilla nose with peatyness and sea air, citrus hints, with vanilla, orange and lemon notes intensifying. Rounded peaty body, with light smoke, citrus and vanilla. Creamy, malty finish with peaty range.

Above
Auchentoshan distillery

AUCHENTOSHAN

Established in 1823, at the foot of the Old Kilpatrick Hills overlooking the river Clyde. The name is Gaelic for 'Corner of the field.' Lowland single malt.

TASTING NOTES – AUCHENTOSHAN

10 year old: melon, lightly malty, grassy aromas with vanilla and chocolate hints. The palate is packed with vanilla, spicy oak, ripe melon and citrus with green and red apple hints. Lightly spicy, creamy, malty, vanilla finish.

Three Wood (Bourbon, Oloroso Sherry, Pedro Ximenez casks): balanced nose with sherried fruit, stewed prunes and raisins, lightly malty, peaty hints. Rich sherried ripeness on the palate with raisiny, vanilla, chocolate, caramel, almond and stewed prunes, light smoke, malt and citrus hints. Rich, raisiny finish with creamy sherried notes.

THE BALVENIE

Founded in 1893 by William Grant, who also founded the neighbouring Glenfiddich distillery in 1886. Speyside single malt.

TASTING NOTES – THE BALVENIE

Founder's Reserve 10 year old: heathered, set honey nose with sherried, fruity spice, garnished with oak. A flourish of honeyed vanilla on the palate, with rounded, rich cooked fruit and hint of malty smoke.

Double Wood 12 year old: sherried aromas extend with peaty, cinnamon, fruity, vanilla custard hints. Creamy, sherried maltiness on the palate with a touch of cinnamon and smoke. Richly creamy, citrus, chocolate, cinnamon finish.

Single Barrel 15 year old: vanilla, set honey, chocolate, cinnamon and coconut aromas laced with peat. Creamy, honeyed vanilla, coconut, cinnamon, chocolate flavours balanced by rich, dried fruit and citrus zest hints. Mellow, malty finish. 50.4% non chill-filtered.

21-year-old Port Wood Finish: rich, rounded grapey Port, nutty aromas extending with vanilla and heather honey. Luscious honeyed palate, hints of raisiny fruit and creamy richness, opening up with butterscotch, dark chocolate, caffe latte, nutmeg and spicy oak. Ripe, dry finish with a hint of set honey and dark chocolate.

Single Barrel 25 year old: citrus zest and fresh animated oak aromas extend with cinnamon, nutmeg, coconut, cocoa, rich orange and honey. Elegant, feather light palate with an initial creaminess opening up with honey, orangey chocolate and citrus zest. Chocolate orange finish. 50.4%abv non chill-filtered.

BENNACHIE

Established in 1998 the company name and the Pure Malt range derive from the Bennachie Mountain in Speyside. Vatted malts.

TASTING NOTES - BENNACHIE

10 year old: rich, lightly sherried nose. Soft palate with initial sherried sweetness, heather and honey. Very long smokey finish.

17 year old: soft, sweet sherried nose. Soft palate with rich sherry delivery. Lightly creamy, malty finish bearing a hint of smoke.

21 year old: hint of musk within the oakey, toasty, lightly spicy nose. Rounded, rich, sherried and vibrant oaky notes, with smokey, malty, creamy notes. Additional malty, creamy, barley, oakey flavours unfolding in the finish.

BENRIACH

Situated in Elgin, Benriach opened in 1898 and was restored in 1965, retaining its distinctive pagoda roof and floor maltings.

TASTING NOTES – BENRIACH

10 year old: lightly peaty, floral aromas with rich vanilla. Elegant vanilla, caramel flavours with rich dried fruit, citrus hint and underlying peat. Delicate malty finish. 43 per cent abv.

BENROMACH

Established in 1898 on the outskirts of the town of Forres, the distillery was purchased by Gordon & MacPhail in 1993. The distinctive, almost 100-foot, red brick chimney is a central feature. Speyside single malt.

Above

Benriach has one of the smallest floor maltings in Scotland.

TASTING NOTES – BENROMACH

12 year old: fruity, chocolate toffee aromas. Cinnamon and dried fruit on the palate. Subtle finish.

BLADNOCH

Scotland's most southerly distillery, founded in the early 19th century. Lowland single malt.

TASTING NOTES - BLADNOCH

10 year old: candied and fresh citrus, lemon zest and lemon juice aromas with underlying malty, biscuity notes. Lemon juice and zest on the palate with vanilla custard/ice-cream, coconut hints and supporting malty, biscuity notes. Zesty lemon finish with malty creaminess. 43 per cent abv.

BLAIR ATHOL

The distillery was established in 1798 in the foothills of the Grampian mountains, 7 miles away from the village of Blair Athol in Perthshire. Highland single malt.

TASTING NOTES - BLAIR ATHOL

12 year old: creamy vanilla custard aromas with soured cream, set honey, nutmeg and gingerbread hints. Luscious, honeyed vanilla palate with light citrus freshness, vanilla custard, nutmeg, gingerbread, coconut and hint of fruitcake. Smooth, mellow finish. 43 per cent abv.

BOWMORE

Established on the shores of Loch Indaal on the island of Islay in 1779 by David Simpson. The traditional floor maltings have been retained, with Islay peat used during kilning. Islay single malt.

TASTING NOTES - BOWMORE

Legend: peaty, seaweed aromas. Smokey, peaty notes on the palate balanced by sweetness. Refreshing, elegant finish.

12 year old: peaty, lemon, sea spray aromas. Smokey, sea spray, chocolatey, fruity, honeyed notes on the palate. Sustained finish.

TASTING NOTES - BOWMORE

15 year old: peaty, smokey vanilla interplay on the nose, laced with maltiness. Creamy, vanilla, chocolate, malty peatyness on the palate with citrus freshness spanning grapefruit and lemon. Fresh release of creamy maltyness with waft of smoke and peat in the finish.

17 year old: malty, peaty, lightly smokey, toasty nose with vanilla and stewed fruit hints. Incredibly delicate palate, yielding vanilla and peat with well-integrated smoke, hint of sea spray and citrus zest freshness. Additional malty release in the finish.

21 year old: peaty, sherried, lemon zest, biscuity aromas with vanilla custard, marzipan and fruitcake hints emerging. Delicate sherried richness with vanilla maltyness, walnut, heather honey, peaty smoke and sea spray, garnished with fresh lemon and a hint of sherried fruitcake. Soft, creamy, malty finish.

1984: continual nuances of light peaty smoke, fresh orange zest, vanilla, cold jasmine tea and jammy richness. Elegant, light peaty smoke on the palate with stewed fruit, prunes, vanilla, dark chocolate, and hints of caffe latte with citrus freshness. Creamy, malty, biscuity, citrus finish, extending with chocolate and vanilla.

BRUICHLADDICH

The most westerly distillery, Bruichladdich was established in 1881 across the Loch Indaal from Bowmore. The distillery was acquired in 2000 by Murray McDavid, an independent Scottish company, making this one of the few independent distilleries in Scotland. It is pronounced 'brook-laddie', Gaelic for 'shore bank'. Single Islay malt.

TASTING NOTES - BRUICHLADDICH

10 year old: peaty, smokey, sea air, briny aromas laced with subtle fruit. Soft mouthfeel with creamy malt, smokey, peaty, set honey and vanilla caramel. Malt, vanilla finish with hint of pungency and waft of smoke.

15 year old: malty, biscuity nose with quite pungent vanilla and caramel, cooked fruit hints. Creamy, biscuity, luscious vanilla palate, and a hint of fruit zest, with layers of vanilla building up throughout.

BUNNAHABHAIN

The distillery was established in 1883, looking across the Sound of Islay to the Paps of Jura. The name, pronounced 'Bu-na-havenn', is Gaelic for 'the mouth of the river.' Islay single malt.

TASTING NOTES - BUNNAHABHAIN

12 year old: rich, balanced medley of smoke and fruity cooked orange aromas. Light elegant flavours emerge from a lightly cooked fruit palate, opening up with creamy malty, smokey hints. Rich rounded finish with rich fruit and malt.

CAOL ILA

Originally built in 1846, the still room's vast picture windows look across the sound of Islay to the dramatic mountains on the neighbouring Isle of Jura. The name, pronounced 'Cull-eela', is Gaelic for 'the sound of Islay'. Islay single malt.

TASTING NOTES - CAOL ILA

15 year old: briny, iodine, marine nose with vanilla, peaty depth. Light, elegant palate with citrus, creamy malt, vanilla and chocolate laced with peaty, smokey hints and gradual build up of creamy richness. Robust finish releasing smokey, malty vanilla.

CARDHU

A rare distillery in the sense that women played a significant role in its evolution. Helen Cumming, the founder's wife, distilled the first batch of whisky herself in 1811. Her daughter-in-law, Elizabeth, took over the distillery in 1872, rebuilding it in 1885 and tripling sales volume within a few years. Highland single malt.

Below

An antique label from Cardhu distillery.

TASTING NOTES - CARDHU

12 year old: spicy oak, malt nose laced with vanilla and caramel. Creamy, elegant palate with biscuity, citrus, orange marmalade, cooked fruit notes with ripe dryness. Finish spans butterscotch, vanilla and fruit hints.

CHIVAS BROTHERS THE CENTURY OF MALTS

Vatted malt comprising 100 single malts from each region, including some distilleries which are no longer operational.

TASTING NOTES - CHIVAS BROTHERS THE CENTURY OF MALTS

Initial TCP aromas, opening up with smokey toffee and rich fruit. Elegantly peaty, smokey palate with citrus hints and rich, dried fruit, extending with balanced interplay between the flavours. Rich, smokey, lingering finish.

CLYNELISH

Established in 1819, this is one of the most northerly distilleries. Highland single malt.

TASTING NOTES - CLYNELISH

14 year old: fruit cake with vanilla creme anglaise and waft of smoke on the nose. Soft, creamy vanilla, coconut, fruit cake palate, with smokey waft. Fresh fruitcake, malty finish. 43 per cent abv.

CRAGGANMORE

Founded in 1869 at the foot of Craggan Mor Hill, from which the stone for the distillery was quarried. Highland single malt.

Below
Cragganmore distillery was one of the first to make use of the new railway system.

TASTING NOTES - CRAGGANMORE

12 year old: lightly oakey, vanilla, malty nose with citrus edge. Elegant palate with creamy, malty, butterscotch, balanced by spice and lemon zest with growing malty, gingerbread, lightly honeyed, dark chocolate and smokiness. Biscuity, lightly smokey finish.

DALLAS DHU

The distillery was built in 1989, and is now a malt whisky museum. Nevertheless, this malt is still available in limited quantities. Highland single malt.

TASTING NOTES - DALLAS DHU

12 year old: honeyed vanilla aromas laced with coconut. Delicate palate with honeyed, creamy vanilla, coconut and biscuit notes, extending with creamier malt. Fresh fruitcake, malty finish.

DALWHINNIE

Opposite
Dalwhinnie
distillery is also
an official
meteorological
station.

The distillery was established in 1897 and is more than 1,000 feet above sea level, on the moors of the Grampian mountains. Accomodation was always provided for employees, as the distillery could be snowbound for days at a time. The name is Gaelic for 'the meeting place'. Highland single malt.

TASTING NOTES - DALWHINNIE

15 year old: fruity, citrus zest aromas, with vanilla, caramel, oakey spice and smokey hints. Subtle peaty, smokey notes on the palate, with creamy, heather honey, fudge notes and citrus freshness. Soft heathery finish. 43 per cent abv.

EDRADOUR

The smallest and one of the most traditional distilleries, virtually unchanged since it was founded in 1825 by local farmers. Resembling a village set around a burn, it is staffed by three men who live in cottages within the grounds. Highland single malt.

TASTING NOTES - EDRADOUR

10 year old: sherried, butterscotch, creamy, vanilla aromas with cafe latte, nutmeg hints. Honeyed, creamy, dried fruits and minty spice on the palate with sherried, lightly smokey dark chocolate overtones. Creamy, rich vanilla creme anglaise finish.

FAMOUS GROUSE

Distilled by Matthew Gloag, The Famous Grouse name is also established as a blend as well as a malt. Vatted malt.

TASTING NOTES - FAMOUS GROUSE

The Famous Grouse Vintage Malt: rich, fruity, sherried, nose. Rounded, yielding palate, with spicy citrus hints. Sustained finish with rich, oakey notes.

GLENFARCLAS

The distillery was established in 1836, at the foot of the Benrinnes mountains. The distillery is a family run business which has been passed down through five generations of the Grant family. Highland single malt.

TASTING NOTES - GLENFARCLAS

10 year old: initial fruit zest opens up with vanilla, nutmeg, coconut and honey, garnished by oakey spice. Silky, initially dry palate opens up with rich vanilla and coconut, with hints of dried fruit and supple spicy oak. Oakey finish garnished with vanilla, cooked fruit and prunes.

15 year old: honeyed vanilla, apple pie and custard aromas, with coconut and ember hints. Dry palate opens up with caramelised apples, vanilla custard, nutmeg and dark chocolate, garnished with lightly oakey smoke.

GLENFIDDICH

Established in 1886 in Speyside by William Grant and his nine sons. The distillery pioneered malt whisky's international emergence by exporting single malt in the 1960s. The name means 'Valley of the Deer' in Gaelic. Highland single malt.

TASTING NOTES - GLENFIDDICH

Special Reserve 12 year old: fresh nose with dried fruit hints and underlying vanilla malt. Creamy vanilla maltyness on the palate with dried fruit, fruitcake, set honey and peaty hints. Rounded, biscuity, malty finish.

Solera Reserve 15 year old: honeyed aromas carry layers of vanilla, gentle spice and fresh fruit. Honeyed palate balanced by coconut, delicate spice and oak. Sustained finish.

Ancient Reserve 18 year old: intense honeyed aromas, with fruity, apple, oakey hints. Soft, malty, oakey notes on the palate balanced by sherried richness, soft vanilla and sultanas. Long honeyed oak finish with a dry conclusion.

30 year old: lightly grassy, pine, herbaceous aromas with smoke, tobacco and richly polished oak hints. Ultra-mellow palate with creamy white chocolate, vanilla ice cream and a rich dried fruit garnish with light malt and baked banana hints. Creamy finish with malt, smokey, baked banana.

40 year old: deep dried fruit, sultana aromas with sherried oakiness, hints of vanilla, cigar leaf, smoke and beeswax polished furniture, with light maltiness. Dry, elegant palate with rounded dried fruit, walnut, creamy malt, smokey, dark chocolate. Chocolate, espresso finish.

GLENGOYNE

Established in 1833, when it was the only one of 13 illicit distilleries in the area to become licensed. The name is thought to derive from the Gaelic for 'Valley of the goose', or 'geese'. Highland single malt.

TASTING NOTES – GLENGOYNE

17 year old: soft vanilla nose with creamy, honeyed, coconut and biscuity hints. Delicate, dry, rich palate with honeyed vanilla, coconut, and a biscuit note, garnished with oakey spice. Animated finish with deep malty, biscuity notes. 43 per cent abv.

GLEN GRANT

Founded in 1840, the distillery's 27-acre woodland garden (open to the public), recently took three years to restore to its Victorian character. This includes a lily pond, bog garden and rustic bridges over the tumbling Back Burn. The son of the founders, Major Grant, took guests for a dram to a special hut on the side of the ravine, drawing water from the burn. Highland single malt.

TASTING NOTES – GLEN GRANT

Glen Grant: elegant vanilla, coconut aromas with hint of ripe fruit. An initially dry palate opens up with rich apricot, peach, pear flavours, coconut and a spicy garnish. Long finish with malty creaminess.

10 year old: vanilla elegance on the nose with a malty, creamy fruit trifle hint. Creamy palate with coconut, dried fruit and vanilla custard with hints of fruit trifle, citrus and zesty orange. Rich, malty finish.

GLENKEITH

The distillery was built in 1958 from local Keith stone, on the site of the historic Keith Mills. Speyside single malt.

TASTING NOTES – GLENKEITH

10 year old: toffee, butterscotch aromas, with vanilla fruit and maltyness. Syrupy, honeyed, creamy, vanilla palate with chocolate malty overtones. Smooth, citrus malty finish.

GLENKINCHIE

Established in 1837, 15 miles from Edinburgh, where the local soil always yielded some of the finest barley. The distillery also features a museum which details the production process. Lowland single malt.

TASTING NOTES – GLENKINCHIE

10 year old: elegant vanilla, coconut aromas laced with biscuity, malt, oakey hints. Creamy, malty, vanilla palate with dried fruit, a hint of butterscotch, spice and citrus, lemon tang. Malt, lemon and chocolate combine in the finish. 43 per cent abv.

THE GLENLIVET

Founded by George Smith, who was the first distiller to take out a licence following the 1823 Excise Act. Highland single malt.

TASTING NOTES – GLENLIVET

12 year old: fresh vanilla, caramel, butterscotch aromas laced with cooked fruit. Delicate texture laden with cooked fruit flavours, a hint of spice, smoke and creamy butterscotch. Subtly spicy finish.

12-year-old French Oak Finish: ripe, spicy, rich vanilla floral nose. Cooked fruit flavours garnished with spicy oak, vanilla custard and fudge with citrus zest. Burst of oakey spice and malt in the finish.

18 year old: sherried, lightly oakey nose, with these notes coming through on the palate accompanied by creamy, lightly fudgey tones.

Glenlivet Archive: fruity, floral elegance on the nose. Rich fruityness on the palate accompanied by creamy, lightly fudgey notes.

GLENLOSSIE

This picturesque distillery was built in 1876 by John Duff, four miles south of Elgin, Morayshire. One of the fire engines, used to quell a serious fire which broke out in 1929 can also be seen there. Speyside single malt.

TASTING NOTES – GLENLOSSIE

Glenlossie 10 year old: linseed oil, humidor nose, with vanilla pod freshness emerging through the heather moor notes. Dry silky palate with a hint of honeyed fruit, gingerbread and lemon notes, with an oakey garnish. Vanilla, creamy malt finish.

GLENMORANGIE

Licensed in 1843, the distillery's workforce is referred to as the 'sixteen men of Tain,' with the company a pioneer of special wood finishes. The name is Gaelic for 'Glen of Tranquility.' Highland single malt.

TASTING NOTES – GLENMORANGIE

10 year old: soft aromas with lightly creamy, butterscotch, fruity, spicy pear, floral and smokey notes. Animated fruit and honey flavours, accented by subtle smoke. Soft finish with butterscotch pear hints.

18 year old: animated, integrated, spicy, nutty, fruity notes with malt, vanilla and ember hints. Elegant palate with ripe, spicy, cooked fruit laced with vanilla, creamy custard and nutmeg, hints of malt, butterscotch and dark chocolate, garnished with spice.

Port Wood Finish: butterscotch, dark chocolate, caramel aromas with a waft of vanilla, spearmint and spiced citrus zest. Velvety palate, balancing richness and dryness, with creamy dark and white chocolate, mocha, caffe latte, and peppermints. Walnuts and port combine in the lasting finish, joined by vanilla and butterscotch hints. 43 per cent abv.

Madeira Wood Finish: fresh citrus zest aromas with charcoal, embers, fortified wine, fruitcake and vanilla hints. Spicy, well integrated flavours remain consistent with vanilla, fruit and citrus zest freshness. Dry finish with citrus and fruit trifle flourishes. 43 per cent abv.

Sherry Wood Finish: full-bodied sherry, nutty, spicy set honey, mead aromas with ember hints. Lightly syrupy palate with full-bodied, balanced flavours spanning subtle creamy maltyness, set honey, nutmeg and dark chocolate. Sherried, walnut finish with honeyed fruitcake and malty hints. 43 per cent abv.

Glen Moray

Located on the banks of the river Lossie in Elgin, on Speyside, Glen Moray, pronounced 'Glen Murray', was established in 1897, converting a former brewery dating from 1815. Speyside single malt.

TASTING NOTES – GLEN MORAY

Speyside Malt Chardonnay barrel finish: light, refreshing aromas with vinous top notes, butterscotch, lemongrass, vanilla and citrus hints. Creamy, malty palate with citrus, pear notes, and a garnish of spicy hints.

12-year-old Chenin Blanc finish: fresh, heather honey, grapey, citrus, grapefruit aromas with toffee, oak hints. Lightly honeyed palate with zesty lemon, citrus, grapefruit, malty, butterscotch, dark chocolate hints and oak garnish. Dry, fruity grapey tang in the malty, chocolate, butterscotch and fudge finish.

16 year old Chenin Blanc finish: complexity develops with the wine's silky fresh notes emerging. Long, dry oakey finish.

Glen Ord

Located on the Black Isle (northwest of Inverness), the distillery was founded in 1838. A long association with The Clan Mackenzie reflects the use of The Clan's motto: 'I shine not burn'. Highland single malt.

TASTING NOTES – GLEN ORD

12 year old: light sherry oak aromas extend with creamy, malty, biscuity, peat hints. Delicate palate with hints of ripe, dried fruit, garnished with oakey spice. Creamy, malty, biscuity finish with dry sherry richness.

23 year old: peaty, smokey nose with hints of vanilla, citrus and toffee apple. Smokey, peaty palate with vanilla, citrus and ripe fruit notes, Rich, luscious, balanced finish.

Above
Glen Ord
distillery.

Glen Scotia

Licensed in 1835, Glen Scotia has retained some of the original buildings and a historic still house. Campbeltown single malt.

TASTING NOTES – GLEN SCOTIA

14 year old: luscious vanilla nose laced with smokey waft, butterscotch and honeyed, creamy malt. Soft palate with a hint of smoke permeating honeyed, butterscotch notes, garnished by sea spray and citrus hints. Malty, butterscotch finish.

The Glenturret

The Glenturret distillery is one of the claimants to the title of the oldest distillery in Scotland. Illicit stills were established on the site from 1717, with the first licensed distillery dating from 1775. Highland single malt.

TASTING NOTES – GLENTURRET

15 year old: rich nose integrating vanilla with subtle oakyness, opening into a rounded waft. Creamy, butterscotch, vanilla palate with hints of chargrilled tropical fruit and pear drops.

HIGHLAND PARK

Scotland's most northerly distillery, established in 1798 on the site of an illicit operation. It is one mile further north than Scapa, the neighbouring distillery on Orkney. The distinctive 'H' emblem was inspired by an illuminated manuscript in St Magnus Cathedral.

TASTING NOTES – HIGHLAND PARK

12 year old: lightly smokey, gingery, spicy nose with sherry, toffee and a hint of cigar and tobacco leaf, balanced by lemony, creamy vanilla. Delicate smooth palate with creamy butterscotch, a smokey hint and refreshing citrus, ginger, cinnamon streak. Hints of dried fruit, chocolate and peaty smoke in the finish.

18 year old: smokey, malty nose with a hint of ginger, spicy oak, dried fruit and Christmas cake hints. Delicate though full-bodied, creamy, citrus palate with hints of nuttiness and cinnamon. Citrus finish with creamy malt.

2000 Limited Edition: citrussy, dried fruit nose with spicy, oakey smoke, laced with creamy sherried vanilla, intensifying with hints of liquorice, and nutty almonds. Smooth palate with light smoke and peat carrying fresh vanilla, lemon and orange, fresh and luscious with oakey sherried hints and rich chocolate. Fresh, ripe but dry, concentrated finish.

ISLE OF JURA

Established in 1810 on the eponymous Isle of Jura, the name stems from Old Norse, possibly meaning the 'island of yew trees' or 'island of red deer'. Highland single malt.

TASTING NOTES – ISLE OF JURA

10 year old: roasted, salted almonds and rich, vanilla egg custard aromas laced with peat. Fruity palate with hints of elegant oilyness, roasted almonds, citrus freshness and smokey hint. Malty finish with light salty, almond, citrus notes.

KNOCKANDO

Established in 1899. The traditional practice of recording the season (year), of production on the bottle continues. The name derives from the Gaelic for 'little black hill.' Highland single malt.

TASTING NOTES – KNOCKANDO

1987: raspberry hints in a fruity, creamy nose with honeyed malt. Elegant palate with light malt, vanilla custard creaminess, coconut hint and spicy oak garnish.

LAGAVULIN

Established in 1816, the distillery overlooks Lagavulin Bay with its 13th-century, romantically ruined Dunyvaig Castle. The name stems from the Gaelic for 'the hollow where the mill is'. Islay single malt.

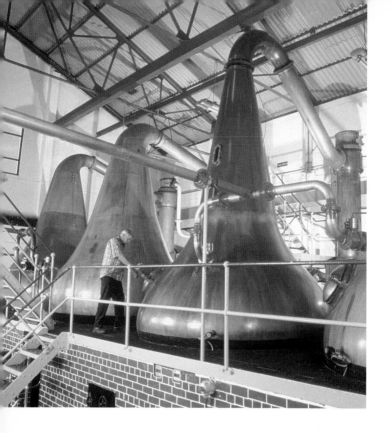

Above
The stills at
Lagavulin.

TASTING NOTES – LAGAVULIN

16 year old: fresh, deep, peaty nose with citrus zest and vanilla hints. Smokey palate laced with creamy, malty, lemon freshness and sea spray hint at the edges. Finish combines smoke, peat, and sea spray hint with creamy malt. 43 per cent abv.

LAPHROAIG

Established in 1815 by local farmers, the name is Gaelic for 'beautiful hollow by the broad bay', which describes its location. Awarded a Royal Warrant by HRH the Prince of Wales. Islay single malt.

TASTING NOTES – LAPHROAIG

10 year old: initial TCP aroma subsides into embers, smokey, 'out by the bonfire' aromas, with iodine, seaweed, briny, vanilla notes. Luscious palate, with smokey, sea spray, citrus, vanilla and coconut layers with fresh, salty lemon. Big creamy, malty finish with gentle, smokey wafts.

15 year old: initial carbolic soap, charcoal combination opens up into TCP, and a wave of marine, seaweed, elegantly oily, citrus zest hints, followed by a burst of sea spray and malty smokiness. Elegant though powerful palate with sea spray, citrus, smokey, peaty, malty flavours, accompanied by dried fruit zest and vanilla custard creaminess, garnished with spicy oak. 43 per cent abv.

30 year old: subtle but rich and rounded, out in the heather moor peatyness on the nose, with vanilla fruit emerging. Incredibly mellow palate, with smooth rounded peat, garnished with smoke, citrus and sea spray.

Above

Laphroig distillery on Islay – historically the remote and rugged shoreline made the area popular with smugglers.

LINKWOOD

Built in 1821 by the river Lossie close to the town of Elgin in Speyside, the picturesque distillery been rebuilt several times and now has two still houses. Speyside single malt.

TASTING NOTES – LINKWOOD

12 year old: malty, vanilla, fudge elegance on the nose with underlying oakey spice and smokey hint. Smooth, luscious vanilla on the palate with hints of oak, spice, dark chocolate, lemon tang, orange zest, orange marmalade, and maltyness. Finishes with peat, malt, biscuit, lemon and chocolate hints. 43 per cent abv.

LITTLEMILL

Established around 1772, by which time houses to accomodate excise officers had already been built, Littlemill is one of the oldest distilleries in Scotland situated at the foot of the Kilpatrick mountains. Lowland single malt.

TASTING NOTES – LITTLEMILL

8 year old: elegant linseed, sunflower oil aromas, with heathery, peaty hints. Elegantly oily palate, garnished with peaty, smokey, vanilla, lemon and oak.

LOCHINDAAL

This malt was introduced in 1989 by Associated Distillers, a privately owned company. Islay single malt.

TASTING NOTES – LOCHINDAAL

10 year old: vanilla, fudge aromas with a hint of smoke and sea air. Ripe, citrussy palate with hint of sea spray and peat. 43 per cent abv.

LONGMORN

The name derives from that of Morgan, a holy man whose chapel once occupied the site of the distillery, which was founded in 1894. Highland single malt.

TASTING NOTES – LONGMORN

15 year old: fruity, vanilla, heather honey, floral bouquet. Luscious, elegant palate with rich, ripe fruit, a hint of citrus zest and chocolate.

THE MACALLAN

Licensed in 1824, malt whisky was distilled at Craigellachie since medieval times. The only single malt to be matured exclusively in Sherry oak casks. Highland single malt.

TASTING NOTES – MACALLAN

10 year old: apple aromas (more red than green apples), extending with apricot, dried fruits, cloves, ginger, toffee and sherry. Smooth, rounded palate with a light apple note, dried cooked fruit, orange zest, spicy cloves, ginger, cinnamon butterscotch and dark chocolate. Well-integrated, rich, dry finish, with sherried, fruity hints.

12 year old: hint of sherried oak, cinnamon, toffee, fudge, vanilla, dried apricot and lemon zest. Indulgent palate with toffee, fudge, fresh lemon zest and juice, extending with orangey hints.

15 year old: sherried aromas integrated with cinnamon and mellow orange zest. Elegant dried fruit flavours extend with apple and orange notes, creamy, oakey spice with fudge and sherry notes. Nutty, toffee finish with spicy orange.

18 year old: spicy nose with cloves, ginger, cinnamon and nutmeg, light smoke, oak and subtle cooked fruit. Pronounced citrus fruits expand on the elegant palate, garnished with a hint of oak and spice.

25 year old Anniversary: sherry and vanilla freshness on the nose with mellow, citrus, dried fruit, ginger and set honey, and lingering oak hint. Silky complexity on the palate with lemon, citrus notes balanced by toffee, fudge, stewed prunes and vanilla custard, and smokey hints. Malty finish.

30 year old: resiny, spicy nose with citrus, orange, rich dried fruit and sherried notes. Spicy sherried richness on the palate with an orange and lemon freshness.

50 year old: rich cooked fruit, prunes and vanilla aromas with a hint of spice, smoke and vanilla custard. Incredibly mellow, luscious palate with lightly smokey, rich fruit flavours, garnished with fruit zest. Rich, ripe finish.

MACDONALDS

This malt shows that relative youthfulness, bottled at a higher strength, can provide a very enjoyable combination.

TASTING NOTES – MACDONALDS GLENCOE 8 YEAR OLD

8 year old: Heathery, malty, vanilla nose with walnuts and fruitcake hints. Creamy, fruitcake, cinnamon palate with cooked fruit, vanilla custard and a spicy oak garnish. 58 per cent abv.

MORTLACH

Mortlach was one of the first Dufftown distilleries to be licensed following the 1823 Excise Act. Speyside single malt.

TASTING NOTES – MORTLACH

15 year old: fresh, honeyed vanilla aromas, with creamy marzipan and warm oak. Oakeyness supports a honeyed, vanilla palate, with hints of cocoa, citrus and lemon curd. Citrus finish.

OBAN

Named after a port on the west Highland coast, the distillery was founded in 1794, predating the town which evolved around it, which explains the High Street location. Highland single malt.

TASTING NOTES – OBAN

14 year old: creamy smoke aromas laced with vanilla and spice. Subtle palate spans malty, biscuity flavours laced with vanilla and smokey hints, garnished with citrus spice. 43 per cent abv.

THE OLD ORIGINAL OLDBURY SHEEP DIP

An amusing name, which some farmers used as an affectionate euphemism for whisky, belies a seriously rewarding dram. Vatted malt.

TASTING NOTES – THE OLD ORIGINAL OLDBURY SHEEP DIP

8 year old: fresh, lightly malty, cereal nose with biscuity, elegantly oily, subtle citrus and ember hints. Light, elegant, palate with rounded, creamy, malty flavours, hint of smoke and a biscuity, lightly citrus hint. Juicy, rich, fresh malty finish.

OLD PULTENEY

The distillery, located in the town of Wick, Caithness, was established in 1826. Highland single malt.

TASTING NOTES – OLD PULTENEY

8 year old: biscuity nose, with hints of linseed oil, citrus and fruity, vanilla custard. Smooth, biscuity, creamy, malty, vanilla palate, garnished with oak.

TASTING NOTES – OLD PULTENEY

8 year old: biscuity nose, with hints of linseed oil, citrus and fruity, vanilla custard. Smooth, biscuity, creamy, malty, vanilla palate, garnished with oak.

12 year old: smokey, richly fruity nose. Rich, raisiny, resin notes on the palate with fruitcake, creamy smoke and malt hints. Big malty finish with light smoke.

15 year old: Cocoa, dark chocolate aromas, hint of boiled milk, with an oakey garnish. Milk chocolate, cafe latte, with a hint of cherries on the palate. Malty, chocolate finish.

PITTYVAICH

Established in 1975 in The Dullan Glen, on the outskirts of Dufftown, Banffshire, it is now a specialised distillery for research purposes. Speyside single malt.

TASTING NOTES – PITTYVAICH

12 year old: lusciously balanced, perfumed nose with vanilla, fruitiness and spice. A spicy, oakey core within the velvety palate yields cooked fruit and lemon zest. 43 per cent abv.

Left
*Pittyvaich
distillery was
founded in the
1970s.*

POIT DHUBH

The name, pronounced 'Potch Ggoo', means
'little black pot', referring to pot stills. Additional
information on the label is also offered in Gaelic.
Vatted malts.

TASTING NOTES – POIT DHUBH

8 year old: vibrant, engaging nose opening up with peaty, malty,
smokey hints. Delicate palate with lightly spicy malt, a hint of biscuity,
barley creaminess, leading to citrus freshness in the finish. 43 per cent
abv, unchill-filtered.

12 year old: lively, fresh creamy, malty nose with vanilla overtones.
Delicate palate with malty, creamy notes expanding with spicy hints
and vanilla. Rich, creamy, malty finish. 43 per cent abv, unchill-
filtered.

21 year old: substantial, fresh malty nose with peat, vanilla, sherried,
stewed fruit hints. Soft palate with sherried, cooked fruit, vanilla, malty
creamy notes with refreshing citrus acidity and a biscuity, spicy hint.
Very creamy, malty, chocolatey finish. 43 per cent abv, unchill-filtered.

ROSEBANK

Established on its present site in 1840 at Camelon on the banks of the Forth and Clyde canals. Lowland single malt.

TASTING NOTES –ROSEBANK

12 year old: fresh, elegant nose with vanilla, set honey, fresh coconut and creamy malt. Elegant, subtle palate with honeyed creamy malt, touch of vanilla custard, garnished with oak and dried fruit. Malty, biscuity finish. 43 per cent abv.

ROYAL BRACKLA

Brackla was founded by Captain Fraser in 1812 and is one of only a few Scottish distilleries entitled to used the term 'Royal'. Permission was given by King William IV in 1835, when Royal Brackla was known as 'The King's Own Whisky'. Highland single malt.

TASTING NOTES – ROYAL BRACKLA

1972: creamy, malty, biscuity nose garnished with smokey oak. Mellow, malty palate with biscuity, creamy vanilla laced with smokey hints. Lightly smokey, malty finish.

ROYAL LOCHNAGAR

One of the smallest in the Highlands, the first distillery was established in 1845. The name reflects the fact that the distillery had a royal appointment to Queen Victoria, King Edward VII and King George V. Highland single malt.

Above

Royal Lochnagar was granted its title after a visit from Queen Victoria in the mid-nineteenth century.

TASTING NOTES –ROYAL LOCHNAGAR

12 year old: cooked fruit aromas with vanilla, biscuity, malty notes and citrus hints. Malty, creamy vanilla on the palate with biscuity undertones and cooked fruit released in a ripe but dry, lightly luscious manner. Creamy, malty finish includes a hint of dark chocolate.

SCAPA

Opened in 1885, Scapa is one of the most northerly distilleries, located on Orkney. Highland single malt.

TASTING NOTES – SCAPA

12 year old: peaty nose with amber hints, opening up with heather honeyed fruit, vanilla waft, citrus and sea spray inhalation. Heather honey expands on the palate with creamy malt, citrus, lemon and sea spray hints, while heather honey keeps resurfacing with fresh nuances and a hint of baked apples with cloves and custard. Big, malty finish.

THE SINGLETON OF AUCHROISK

The Auchroisk distillery was opened in 1974 in Banffshire, set on the banks of the river Spey. Highland single malt.

TASTING NOTES – THE SINGLETON OF AUCHROISK

10 year old: elegant nose with wafts of vanilla and butterscotch. Palate opens with ripe, creamy richness, butterscotch, cooked fruit, a hint of dark chocolate and luscious vanilla. Mellow, lively finish with creamy, toffee, dark chocolate hints.

12 year old: vanilla hints laced with cooked fruit and spicy oak on the nose. Creamy, elegant palate with fruity, citrus hints at the edges with subtle vanilla, caramel notes. Ripe, dry finish delivers creamy malt.

SPRINGBANK

Founded in 1828, the distillery is still wholly-owned by the same family, and remains one of the most traditional in its production methods. Campbeltown single malt.

TASTING NOTES –SPRINGBANK

10 year old: vanilla custard, fruit trifle aromas laced with smokey hints. Dark chocolate, cocoa and creamy malt hints animate the fruit trifle, vanilla custard palate. Malty vanilla finish.

21 year old: heathery, peaty, 'windswept heather moor,' aromas with smokey hints permeating vanilla, butterscotch, and fruit cake notes. Supple palate with vanilla, citrus, biscuity malt and fruitcake, rich, ripe and fresh, garnished with spicy oak. Malty, lightly citrus, fruitcake finish. 46 per cent abv.

25 year old: oakey, citrus, pear drop, seaspray aromas with fruitcake hints. Smooth, mellow palate with coconut, fruitcake and refreshing citrus, sea spray tang, a light oak, butterscotch and creamy vanilla garnish. Rich finish with fruitcake, malty, butterscotch notes.

STRATHISLA

Founded in 1786 on the site of a brewery operated by Dominican monks from the 13th century. Highland single malt.

12 year old: spicy, fruity nose with a toffee hint. Medium-bodied, fruity, lightly creamy, lightly luscious palate with citrus hints. Nutty, spicy finish.

TALISKER

Above
Strathisla's
spirit safe.

The Isle of Skye's only distillery, established in 1830 on the shores of Loch Harport. The name derives from the Old Norse 'Thalas Gair,' meaning 'Sloping Rock', referring to the mountains rising behind Talisker House, the traditional home of the Clan Macleod chief's eldest son and leased by the founder of the distillery. Highland single malt.

TASTING NOTES –TALISKER

10 year old: initial lightly peaty, smokey aromas open up with malt, vanilla and citrus zest. Elegant, full-bodied palate with peaty, vanilla, lightly creamy notes with a citrus, sea salt garnish. Rounded, malty, lightly sea salt, smokey finish. 45.8 per cent abv.

TOBERMORY

Established in 1823, it is the Isle of Mull's only distillery, and one of the few independent distilleries, being owned by Burn Stewart Distillers.

TASTING NOTES –TOBERMORY

Fresh vanilla laced with malty hints. Creamy vanilla palate with seamlessly integrated malty, flavours, evolving with hints of vanilla and custard. Creamy, malty vanilla finish provides a rounded conclusion.

TOMATIN

One of the largest malt distilleries and also one of the highest in Scotland, Tomatin (pronounced to rhyme with 'satin') was established in 1897. Highland single malt.

TASTING NOTES –TOMATIN

Vanilla, butterscotch, custard trifle aromas laced with smoke, mellow malt, fruitcake hints and lemon zest. Light honeyed vanilla, vanilla custard, butterscotch flavours with a tiny hint of peat smoke, retains freshness throughout, garnished with a hint of spicy oak.

JOHNNIE WALKER PURE MALT

John Walker opened a grocers shop in 1820 from which he sold a house blend – Walker's Kilmarnock whisky. This evolved into a successful range of blended Scotches together with this vatted malt.

TASTING NOTES –JOHNNIE WALKER

Pure Malt 15 year old: elegant vanilla aromas with light biscuit, dried fruit and Christmas cake hints. Lusciously textured palate with dried, but perky fruit and Christmas cake notes, laced with vanilla, caramel and creamy maltyness. Long, creamy finish with malty, honeyed, dried fruit and further malt flavours opening up.

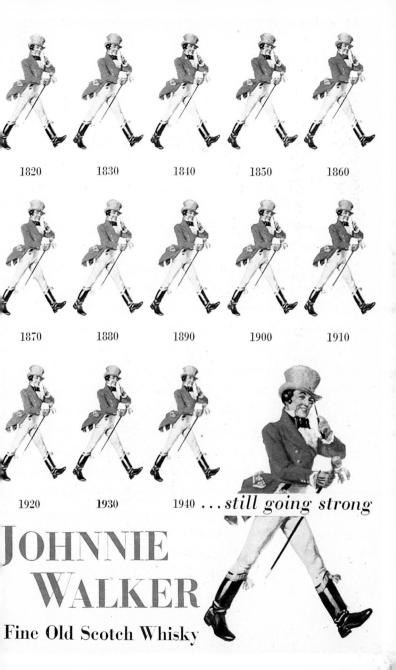

LIQUEURS

COCK O'THE NORTH

Opposite
An historic
Drambuie
advert.

Malt whisky blended with blaeberry (bilberries), and a secret ingredient known only to its creator, the Marquis of Huntly and his son the Earl of Aboyne, descended from the Duke of Gordon who sponsored an Act of Parliament in 1823 to reform whisky distilling in Scotland. The recipe is based on a traditional legend, when it was offered to men in battle and on long journeys.

TASTING NOTES – COCK O'THE NORTH

Rich, ripe fruit and malty aromas, with orange zest, heather honey hints. Lightly syrupy, luscious texture with ripe fruit, lightly orangey top notes, with underlying malty richness. Ripe fruity, fruitcake, fruit trifle finish.

DRAMBUIE

Chronicled as the personal liqueur of Prince Charles Edward Stuart, known as Bonnie Prince Charlie. He gave his secret recipe to the Mackinnon family who sheltered him on Skye, after being defeated at the Battle of Culloden in 1746. The recipe was commercialised by family descendants in 1909.

TASTING NOTES – DRAMBUIE

Fruity rich orange zest aromas with rounded, malty, chocolate, vanilla notes. Syrupy palate with rich cooked orange, orange zest/juice palate, with a hint of orangey fruit trifle and vanilla custard. Ripe but dry orangey finish.

DRAMBUIE CREAM

A blend of 15–17-year-old malts, fresh cream and heather honey. The name Drambuie is a phonetic version of *'dram buideach'* which means the dram which satisfies.

TASTING NOTES – DRAMBUIE CREAM

Creamy aromas with hints of vanilla, custard and orange zest. Creamy rich palate with zesty orangey, raisiny, vanilla custard, fruit trifle hints. Clean but creamy, zesty vanilla finish.

GLENFIDDICH MALT WHISKY LIQUEUR

Utilising Glenfiddich malt whisky, this liqueur was launched in 1998 by Wm Grant and sons.

TASTING NOTES – GLENFIDDICH MALT WHISKY LIQUEUR

Elegant, subtle nose with a waft of zesty, ripe fruit fruitcake and a hint of oak. Silky texture with malty notes laced with zesty fruit flavours, retaining zesty, citrus freshness and creamy hint. Fresh, citrus, zesty fruitcake finish with hints of creamy vanilla.

STAG'S BREATH

Stag's Breath: originally served as a toast at Hogmanay by local hoteliers in Newtonmore, a village where the liqueur has been produced since 1989. It is a blend of Speyside whiskies and fermented honey comb.

TASTING NOTES – STAG'S BREATH

Light and dry with a distinctive musky nose, and overtaste of the honey's waxy comb.

Malt Whisky Culture

Malt whisky was traditionally drunk down in one from a quaich, but only after proposing a toast. The quaich, derived from the Gaelic *cuach*, meaning a cup or bowl, was a shallow wooden vessel first used in the late 16th century. More ornamental examples followed, comprising staves of different types of wood or horn, bound with a silver rim. A silver disc set into the base of the quaich was also engraved with Gaelic mottos, such as *squab as e*, literally 'clean it out' (ie. down it in one), or *muncuairte* meaning 'pass it around'.

Larger quaichs were used as a 'cup of friendship', which meant taking a sip and passing it on, using the 'lugs' (handles), on each side. A popular theory explaining the addition of handles is that when opposing clan chiefs drank a reconciliatory dram, having both hands occupied indicated that the clansman was not about to draw a weapon (at least, not at the moment of drinking).

Historic alternatives found in coastal areas included a scallop shell (nature's own quaich), and a coconut cup. This 17th-century favourite comprised a coconut either halved or with the top sliced off, mounted on a silver stand.

Opposite
An historic advert for Royal Lochnagar.

Above and opposite
Vessels used to serve whisky. The original quaichs used to serve whisky in the 16th century were shallow wooden bowls.

From the late 17th century, quaichs were fashioned from silver or gold, and typically engraved with roses and tulips. In the early 19th century, when glass was increasingly manufactured and less expensive, tumblers began to replace the quaich for everyday drinking. While gaining in popularity as a present and trophy at sporting events, the quaich was soon reserved for formal occasions; a role it has continued.

Raising a glass to propose a toast, either a tumbler, small goblet or tulip-shaped glass, means repeating *slainte mhor* (Gaelic for 'good health'), or *slainte mhorag* (literally 'to your bigger,' or 'even better health'), which are typically abbreviated to slainte.

Concluding a toast with a theatrical ritual known as 'firing,' reached a peak of popularity in the mid-18th century. After knocking back the malt, the glass was slammed down on the table top, producing a sound that resembled gunfire. This explains why a firing glass had a much thicker base than usual, ensuring it lasted beyond the inaugural use.

While malt whisky was originally drunk neat in Scotland, adding still spring water is a long established custom, with lighter malts popular as an aperitif and richer styles a digestif.

A favourite combination among more mature customers in Scottish pubs is 'a half and a half pint', meaning a single measure of malt accompanied by half a pint of beer. A variation is 'a glass and a pony', a shot glass of mild beer alongside a shot glass of malt. A 'nip and a chaser' follows the same principle, except the emphasis is on effect rather than flavour; the malt being downed in one, with an accompanying pint of beer sipped more leisurely.

Among the few examples of malt being mixed, is a whisky mac (adding ginger wine), a hot toddy (adding boiling water with the likes of sugar, honey and cinnamon) which is a popular restorative; Gaelic coffee (a dram in black coffee or coffee with cream), punch, and Atholl Brose.

Punch typically included heather honey and blaeberries (bilberries), to sweeten what was originally a robust spirit, and often served in a loving cup. This resembled an elegant, decoratively engraved, glass goblet, passed between guests who each took a sip. Punch reached Scotland from India, via England, with the original definition of the Hindu *panch*, meaning 'five', referring to the number of ingredients used: sugar, lime juice, spices, water and alcohol.

Preparing Atholl Brose requires the use of another Scottish staple, oatmeal. This is combined with water to form a paste, which is squeezed through a strainer and the resulting water blended with honey and malt whisky. Atholl Brose dates from 1457 and is named after the Duke of Atholl. He devised a cunning plan to capture his enemy the Earl of Ross. Filling a well, from which the Earl was known to drink water, with Atholl Brose, the Duke watched from a discreet position. The Earl enjoyed the Atholl Brose so much, that once under its spell, his defences were down.

ANNUAL CELEBRATIONS

Right

A Scottish pipe band walking the Royal Mile in Edinburgh.

According to Scottish legend, (always an authoritative start) enjoying a fine whisky entails the additional benefit of hearing a piper playing. Moreover, this accompaniment operates on a

sliding scale. If the whisky is mild, you may hear two pipers; three or four if the whisky is smooth; five or six pipers if it is mellow, while a superlative malt is accompanied by a fully orchestrated 100 Pipers.

Meanwhile, various Scottish celebrations throughout the year mean that pipers really can be heard while enjoying malt whisky.

Hogmanay (New Year's Eve), traditionally entails an 'open house' approach to revellers, but practicalities preceede the celebrations. This means allowing the fire to burn down before midnight, and cleaning out the hearth – with a new fire ready to be lit when midnight strikes. Another tradition is settling debts, in order to start the new year with a clean balance sheet.

'First Footing' refers to the first guest's foot to cross the threshold after the midnight chimes, and to stand over the hearth. This should be a tall, dark and handsome guest to ensure good luck in the coming year. The word 'hogmanay' originally meant gift, and the first footer was expected to bring something to eat, such as fruit or Black Bun (rich fruit cake encased in pastry), something to drink, preferably malt whisky, and a lump of coal representing heat. A first footer arriving without a gift indicated poverty and was taken as an omen that this condition would befall the hosts. Arriving with a silver coin, representing prosperity, got the celebrations off to a much better start.

Whoever ends up standing in front of the hearth, the New Year's toast is proposed with whisky, and throwing the cork from the bottle onto the fire is also customary in the Highlands. The guest offers the host a dram and takes the bottle to the next household. A 19th-century favourite to toast the New Year was Het Pint, a combination of malt whisky, ale and nutmeg, served mulled.

Ne'er Day dinner, on the following day, means another round of malt whisky to accompany traditional fare such as clootie dumpling – a rich plum pudding baked in a cloth (cloot). A more contemporary menu is Scotch broth, haggis (oats, onion, offal and spices encased in a sheep's stomach), goose or steak pie and atholl brose (adding oatmeal and cream converts it into a dessert format), followed by oatcakes with cheese.

Opposite
The Hogmany
Lights over
Edinburgh
Castle and
Princes Street.

Opposite
A scramble
for the Ba' on
New Year's Day
on Orkney.

A cherished tradition on Orkney on New Year's Day is The Ba' (meaning 'ball'). A type of football match, this is contested in the streets of Kirkwall by around 200 men. Competitors and spectators are fortified throughout the match, which can last several hours, by passing hip flasks of malt whisky. Players join the uppie or downie teams, depending on which part of the island they were born: either uptown or downtown from St Magnus cathedral.

The match begins with the eponymous ba', a ball comprising eight leather panels sewn around a piece of cork, being thrown up into the air. Both teams then aim to get the ba' into each others' goal. For the downies, this means the water of the harbour, with uppies heading for a designated wall equidistant from the cathedral. Shoving and even smuggling the ball is perfectly acceptable, as there are no rules to fall foul of.

A player from the winning team is chosen to keep the highly prized ba'. Then celebrations revolve around malt whisky and the ocassional chaser of beer, not to mention the victors jumping off the pier.

During the game, shop fronts are generally protected with wooden bars, while the hospital's casualty department tends to see a few more people than usual. A ladies Ba' was inaugurated in the 1950s, but only two were held. This didn't

reflect a lack of interest. The women competed so intensely that it was stopped for being too aggressive.

Among the various legends explaining the origins of the Ba', the most popular one may also reflect the fact that it is the most grotesque. Apparently, a murderer fleeing the mainland rowed to Orkney, hoping to find refuge. However, the locals rumbled him, and an unofficial jury delivered a guilty verdict. The sentence was decapitation, and kicking the head around the streets of Kirkwall quite naturally evolved into the Ba'.

MALT AND THE MUSE

Burn's Night on January 25 celebrates the birthday of Scotland's national poet, Robert Burns (1759–1796). Burns' poetic works reflected his various love affairs, and one entitled *Scotch Drink* revealed his love affair with whisky: 'O thou, my Muse ! guid auld Scotch drink ... Inspire me, till I lisp an' wink, To sing thy name!' He also had a professional interest in malt to boost his 'poetic' income, and worked shifts as an exciseman, collecting taxes from whisky distillers.

Below
Piping in the Haggis at a Burns Night celebration.

The Burn's Night menu begins with cock-a-leekie soup (chicken and leek), or Scotch broth, followed by haggis with champit tatties (mashed potatoes), and neeps (mashed turnip). The haggis makes an impressive spectacle, held reverentially

on a silver salver as the chef takes it around the dining room with a full musical accompaniment from a piper, who is rewarded with a double dram. Reciting Burns' *Address to the Haggis*, including the thoroughly deserved accolade, 'Great chieftain o' the puddin' race', preceedes the ceremonial slicing of the haggis using a sword. A dram is sometimes poured over the haggis.

A beef or venison dish may follow, while pudding is either

Left
*The monument
to Robert Burns
in Ayrshire.*

trifle flavoured with whisky, instead of the usual sherry or atholl brose. Dinner concludes with bannocks and kebbuck, (hard cheeses and oatcakes).

Malt whisky is served throughout the dinner, which acts as a forum for speeches and recitals in praise of Himself. Verses from *Tam O'Shanter* are essential as this is considered the ultimate work to recite, while *The Immortal Memory*, a speech celebrating Burns' achievements, forms the centrepiece of the evening. The success of a Burn's Night (traditionally an all-male event), rests on the speakers' ability to dramatise with a carefully structured order.

And after all that reciting, it makes a nice change to sing some songs, also penned by Burns. This culminates in *Auld Lang Syne*, literally 'The Good Old Days', within which the 'cup of kindness' refers to malt whisky as the spirit of friendship.

The evening can extend with a *ceilidh*, originally a social gathering for songs and storytelling, which now refers to Scottish music and dancing. Traditionally salted herring and potatoes were served at a ceilidh, accompanied by malt whisky. Although this has long been replaced by a helping of stoavies (lamb, potatoes and onions cooked in a large pot), the accompaniment remains the same.

A SPORTING CHANCE

A hip flask of malt whisky is an essential accessory at various sporting occasions in Scotland, such as shooting, hunting, stalking and fishing. The start of the angling season in February is marked by a more ceremonial session at the river Spey and river Tey. A piper leads a procession of anglers to the river bank, where a few words are repeated by a guest of honour. This includes a general welcome, wishing everyone 'a tight line' (ie. good luck), and perhaps a request to the fish to take the bait more readily. While a minister of the Kirk may bless the river, it is also 'annointed' with malt whisky, poured from the river bank or from a boat in the middle of the river. The anglers and piper then toast the river with a dram, having already enjoyed one on arrival.

Hospitality tents dispense an abundance of malt whisky at Highland Games, which are held between May and September at more than 70 locations throughout Scotland. Dating back at least 1,000 years, the origins of Highland Games are entirely practical. Highland chiefs recruiting to their entourage had an ideal opportunity to discover who was the fastest and strongest. The 11th-century King Malcolm Canmore, for example, founded the first hill race in Royal Deeside, in order to recruit the fastest messenger.

Tossing the caber is considered a feat of strength, but it actually requires enormous skill, the caber being an 18 foot, 150 lb tree trunk of native pine. Style rather than distance is the award-winning element, particularly as the caber

Below
Throwing the hammer at the games in Stirling.

must land in the 12 o'clock position, having attained a 180 degree arc *en route*. Displays of pipe bands and Highland dancing also animate the festivities.

MALT AND LOVE

In addition to the minister, another vital person at a Scottish wedding is a piper, who traditionally leads the bride and groom into and out of church, as well as to the wedding reception. The piper's fee takes the form of drams during the reception and a bottle to enjoy at home.

On Orkney, toasting the newly-weds involves a wedding cog at receptions, (and beyond if an Orcadian couple marry 'overseas'). This small wooden cask resembles the bottom half of a barrel, with a pair of flat or turned handles. Orkney does of course have specialist cog makers, with more ornamental examples combining various types of wood, while a silver plate on the cog is engraved with the couple's name and wedding date.

The couple usually receive a wedding cog as a present from a close friend, who may also provide alcohol to fill the cog. This can be quite an undertaking, with a typical cog having a capacity of about five pints (though larger and smaller versions do exist). This means plenty of malt whisky, combined with rum, gin, port, ale and

stout, sometimes garnished with nutmeg or cinnamon. While recipes vary, brown sugar and gentle heating (it is served hot but not boiled) are instrumental in linking the flavours. After the wedding meal, and once the bride and groom have had their first dance, they take the wedding cog to each group of guests, beginning with their families. Everyone takes a sip from the cog while congratulating the couple. The bestman and chief bridesmaid then provide another round by following with their own cog.

A groom on Orkney, and other parts of Scotland, may already have had his fill of malt

Below
A wedding cog from Orkney. The cog is usually given to the couple by a close friend who often also provides alcohol to fill the cog.

whisky shortly before the wedding ceremony, if subjected to the traditional ritual known as blackening. This sees friends cover the groom in anything black: treacle being the most effective, and cocoa-powder the most user-friendly. The groom may also be stripped for more extensive coverage, with wood shavings added as an effective garnish. Some professions provide their own related substances, with a distillery worker traditionally covered in pot ale (the residue from distillation), while a mechanic is subjected to oil and grease.

The blackened groom then embarks on a pub crawl with friends, involving an abundance of malt whisky. Depending on the blackening agent used, the groom may arrive for the wedding ceremony looking off-white, and sporting a radically short haircut.

On Islay, the bride and groom undergo a similar experience known as pasting. Both are lured to a *rendezvous* with friends, who promptly tie them into the back of a lorry or agricultural trailer. If they cannot be pasted together, friends will compromise and do them separately, which means liberal amounts of cooking oil, eggs, flour and treacle. They are driven around the island in this condition, followed by a convoy of tooting cars, enjoying malt whisky on the way. During the summer, this ritual can culminate in the pasted party being thrown off a pier.

ALL IN A DAY'S WORK

Traditionally distillery employees enjoyed a taste of what they were producing throughout the day, standing in what was known as the dram queue, in order to receive complimentary 'refreshments.' But it wasn't a free for all, as this only applied to employees aged 18 or over.

From a copper jug, the brewer (foreman or distillery manager), poured new make spirit into each employees dram cup. Made of horn or copper, this typically held around 50 ml, with the new make spirit of around 70 per cent abv referred to as spike or white lightning. A Gaelic term *clearic*, reflected the clarity of the spirit. The dram went straight down the hatch in front of the brewer, as taking it off the premises was forbidden, and followed by a chaser of water, as preferred.

Clocking on at the start of a shift, around 7.45 or 8 a.m., also meant joining the first dram queue. Further rounds may have followed around noon and mid-afternoon, plus one for the road before going home. A ruse for an additional dram was quickly rejoining the end of the dram queue, perhaps wearing a different jacket as a decoy. Night shift staff were not forgotten, with miniatures of new make spirit left in their lockers.

Ocassionally the three drams of new make spirit during the day culminated in a dram of aged malt whisky at the end of the shift, a sequence referred to in Perthshire as 'three whites and a goldie.'

Bonus drams could be earned by doing favours, such as washing the distillery manager's car, or undertaking more demanding tasks such as rolling barrels from the warehouse and turning barley on the malting floor.

The manner in which a bonus dram was earned also yielded its own vocabulary, with a 'stoodie' ('dusty') dram for sweeping out a dusty area. A 'dirty' dram referred to a dirty job such as cleaning out the boilers, while painting the top of the warehouse was clearly a 'double dram' job, resulting in a 'stoater' ('a big one').

The distillery manager also gave the cooper a celebratory dram on completing his apprenticeship which lasted around four years. This rites of passage meant getting the cooper down to his underwear, blackening him with treacle, wood shavings and charcoal taken from the interiors of charred casks, then rolling him around the cooperage inside a hogshead cask, (capacity around 250 litres, with the head and end removed). Sometimes the journey extended round the local village. Once cleaned up, a malt whisky session ensued at the local pub.

Distillery employees weren't the only beneficiaries of the dramming system, with visiting tradesmen and suppliers also joining the dram queue. This included the crew of puffers, the small ships bringing supplies and taking

whisky from the islands to the mainland. **Above**
Similarly, deliveries of coal resulted in a dram for *Distillery staff*
the coalmen. In fact, as distilleries operated *at Aberlour*
slightly different dramming timetables, some *in the early*
tradesmen were known to do a circuit, arriving at *twentieth*
a distillery just in time for the next dram queue. *century.*
Even tradesmen totally unconnected with the
distillery tried their luck in the dram queue, and
were often successful.

When the practice of dramming began is
uncertain, but the Articles of Agreement posted
at a Speyside distillery in 1878, states: 'drams may
be given to the men as an indulgence, but they
cannot be claimed as a right.' When the dram

queue and associated customs ended is more precise. Health and Safety Regulations in 1978 prohibited the consumption of alcohol while working. However, many distilleries adapted the tradition, by giving employees a bottle of aged malt whisky each month to take home; a practice which some distilleries have maintained.

One reason for the dram queue was to supplement what were historically modest wages, but another reason may have been to discourage the possibility of pilfering. However, some employees did in the distant past supplement their dram queue allowance, smuggling whisky out of the aging warehouses. Not that perpetrators considered this an infringement, reflecting a popular saying 'freedom and whisky go together', which paraphrased Robert Burns' line, 'freedom and whisky gang thegither'. Exemplifying this, employees could leave pay packets on a table without any anxiety, but not a dram.

Regular trips to the aging warehouse to check for leaking barrels were a prime opportunity for an employee so inclined. An ingenious accessory was a length of copper pipe, typically holding around 3–4 fl oz, and sealed at one end by soldering on a copper penny. Secreted in the trouser leg, it was held in place by a length of string, attached around the neck or to the waistband. For greater discretion, an employee would request dungarees or an overall a couple of sizes too big. While a colleague checked that neither the distillery manager nor excisemen were around, the bung was removed from a barrel, the pipe lowered on a piece of string, filled up, removed, the bung replaced, and the pipe lowered safely back in the trouser leg.

Another option was a 'breaster,' a copper breastplate fashioned by a blacksmith (sympathetic to the cause) and worn under dungarees or an overall. Its capacity was limited to around a pint. Any more, and it would have created a suspicious cleavage.

In addition to tailor-made accessories, everyday items could serve alternative roles once inside the aging warehouse. Hot water bottles nestling down the front of the trousers, were filled with an equally warming liquid. Similarly, a certain brand of salad cream was cherished on Islay, an island not known for its salads. And the reason? The jar's wide neck enabled it to be filled with whisky very quickly, once it was lowered into the barrel on a piece of string.

Any vessel used to remove whisky from a barrel was collectively known as a 'dog', hence the management phrase 'don't take a dog into the warehouse.' While management knew there were dogs on the premises, catching any dog handlers in the act was another matter. Moreover, when whisky was liberated for personal consumption, it could be tolerated. However, if taken for resale the management would get heavy, the consequences being dismissal.

Earlier stages of the production process also, historically, provided employees with opportunities. A popular cold cure in Perthshire was a dram of new make spirit in a cup of the first water from mashing (see page 37) while it was still hot. Needless to say, persistent symptoms may have required regular doses. Another option, known as besem jane, meant taking some of the first water from the mash tun and allowing it to ferment for a day or two, within the privacy of a concealed bucket. Serious drinkers were also known to sink a glass of wash (see page 44), traditionally known as jo. However, employees had to bid jo goodbye in 1946, when Customs & Excisemen started to padlock the hatch to the washbacks.

SERVING MALT WHISKY

Still spring water is added to malt whisky on the basis that it 'opens up' the flavours and aromas, which implies that the existing characteristics become more accessible. However, adding water can significantly alter the flavour profile and mouthfeel. The obvious reason for this is the change in alcoholic strength, which in turn alters the sequence of characteristics revealed by the malt. Whether this is an improvement is obviously a personal decision.

An eight-year-old malt sampled neat, for example, showing vanilla, caramel, spicy honey and citrus zest, with a creamy vanilla finish, displayed a different range when diluted. The palate saw honey and vanilla laced with peaty smoke and hints of parma violets, accompanied by maltier, cereal notes, and a creamier, fuller-bodied malt finish.

The same malt sampled neat as a 12 year old, showed vanilla custard, caramelised apples, toffee and fudge flavours with an oakey, citrus garnish. When diluted, citrus zest came to the fore, accompanied by more substantial creamy, malt notes bearing oakey hints.

Although my personal rule is 'no water', I like malts on the rocks, which can also promote a different range of characteristics, reflecting the change of temperature and a degree of dilution. A

Above
The size and shape of the glass can have a significant impact on the character of the malt.

173

neat 15-year-old malt delivering creamy, biscuity and lusciously unfolding vanilla flavours, garnished by fruit zest, developed a vanilla, caffe latte, mocha, dark chocolate, caramel and fudge palate, garnished with light oak, when retasted on the rocks.

The type of glass used can also influence the character of the malt. The Riedel malt whisky glass was developed in Scotland in conjunction with master distillers. Taking the form of an elongated thistle shape on a truncated stem, a small lip directs spirit onto the tip of the tongue, where sweetness is perceived, emphasising its creaminess.

Nosing a 10-year-old malt in a similarly proportioned, chimney-shaped glass, the aromas amounted to hints of spice and honey, with mild vanilla and spiced fruit flavours culminating in a subdued finish. The nose was far more rewarding in the Riedel glass, with elegant vanilla, honey and sherried spice, while a smoother, rounder palate featured richer, fruitier, sherried, honey notes and a malty, creamy finish.

Comparing another malt in two alternative glasses, a tulip-shaped glass yielded fresh, lush vanilla notes laced with coconut, pear drops, set honey and a hint of cereal. Nosed in a tumbler, the aromas were milder and slightly less focused, although they also entailed slightly less alcohol. The palate seemed rounder and drier from the tulip glass, while the tumbler emphasised the malt notes and creaminess.

SERVING MALT AROUND THE WORLD

In addition to following the Scottish lead (drinking malt neat or with still spring water), an emerging international trend is to serve a separate glass of still spring water alongside a glass of malt, and to take alternate sips.

In France, malt is drunk neat as an aperitif or digestif, while Italians add water, ice and even mixers. In the USA, malt is typically served on the rocks, with malt whisky and cigars a popular pairing.

Among Asians, Koreans take malt whisky neat, while the Japanese have two additional preferences: on the rocks, and *mizuwari*, which means two and a half parts spring water to one part malt, and ice, stirred at least ten times. This is drunk as a digestif, and also accompanies late night karaoke sessions. Another tradition is for friends to order malt whisky a bottle at a time, and if not finished that evening, the barman keeps the bottle behind the counter, ready for their next visit. Although this practice has declined since the 1980s, and been replaced with a 'by the glass' approach, if you visit Japan and would like to follow suit, its still not difficult to locate bars that will keep the bottle for you – until the next time.

IT TRAVELS WELL

Gazetteer

The Scotch Whisky Association, 20 Atholl Crescent, Edinburgh, EH3 8HF.
Tel: 0131 222 92000.

The Scotch Malt Whisky Society, The Vaults, 87 Giles Street, Edinburgh, EH6 6BZ.
Tel: 0131 554 3451.

Speyside Cooperage Visitor Centre, Dufftown Road, Craigellachie, Banffshire, AB38 9RS.
Tel: 01340 871108.

The Spirit of Speyside Whisky Festival, for information call Elgin Tourist Information Centre, 17 High Street, Elgin IV30 1EG.
Tel: 01343 542666.

Hebridean Island Cruises Ltd (cruises around Scotland and distillery visits), Griffin House, Broughton Hall, Skipton, North Yorkshire, BD23 3AN. Tel: 01756 704704.

SELECTED MALT WHISKY VENUES AND RETAILERS IN SCOTLAND

The Bar, Gleneagles Hotel, Auchterarder, Perthshire.

Chisholms Bar, The Caledonian Hotel, Princes Street, Edinburgh.

The Lobby Bar, Sheraton Grand Hotel, 1 Festival Square, Edinburgh.

The Road Hole Bar, The Old Course Hotel Golf Resort & Spa, St Andrews, Kingdom of Fife.

Quaich Bar, Craigellachie Hotel, Speyside, Banffshire.

Ailsa Bar, Turnberry Hotel, Ayrshire.

Royal Mile Whiskies, 379 High Street, The Royal Mile, Edinburgh.

Loch Fyne Whiskies, Main Street, Inverary, Fife.

Luvians, 93 Bonny Gate, Cupar, Fife, and 66 Markets Street, St Andrews.

SELECTED MALT WHISKY VENUES AND RETAILERS IN ENGLAND

Boisdale, 15 Eccleston Street, London, SW1.

Churchill Bar & Cigar Divan, The Churchill Inter-Continental 30 Portman Square London, W1.

The Malt Whisky Bar, Athenaeum Hotel, 116 Piccadilly, London, W1.

Lanes Cocktail Bar, Four Seasons Hotel, Hamilton Place, London, W1.

The American Bar, The Savoy, Strand, London, WC.2

Green's, 36 Duke Street, St James's, London, SW1.

Cadenhead's Covent Garden Whisky Shop, 3 Russell Street, London, WC2.

Milroys of Soho, 3 Greek Street, London, W1.

Vintage Hallmark of St James's, 36 St James's Street, London SW1.

The Vintage House, 42 Old Compton Street, London, W1.

The Whisky Chaser, 30–34 Wood Street, St Anne's on Sea, Lancashire.

Constantine Stores, 30 Fore Street, Constantine, Falmouth, Cornwall.

SH Jones, 121 Regent Street, Leamington Spa; 27 High Street, Banbury; 8–9 Market Square, Bicester.

BELGIUM (retail) Bacchus, Lippenslaan 13–15, Knokke.

DENMARK
Knut's Karport Bar, Oster
Farimagsgade 12,
Copenhagen.

FRANCE:
The Pure Malt,
4 rue Caron, Paris.

Le Forum, 4 Boulevard
Malesherbes, Paris.

The Auld Alliance Scottish
Pub, 80 rue Francois Miron
Paris.

La Maison du Whisky,
20 rue d'Anjou, Paris.

SWEDEN
Akkurat Restaurant,
Hornsgatan 20, Stockholm.

USA
Whiskey Blue, W New York,
541 Lexington Avenue,
New York.

King Cole Bar, The St Regis
New York, 2 East 55th Street
at Fifth Avenue, New York.

Compass Rose Bar, Westin
St Francis, Union Square,
335 Powell Street,
San Francisco.

The Bar, Blantyre Hotel,
Blantyre Road, Lenox,
Massachussetts.

JORDAN
The Library Bar and Cigar
Lounge, Amman Marriot
Hotel, Issam Ajlouni Street,
Amman.

JAPAN
Malt House 'Bowmore,'
Second Floor, Azabu
Empire, 4–11–28 Nishi-
Azabu, Minato-ku, Tokyo.

Bar Harbour Inn, Third
Floor, Marche Shibata,
1–3–7 Shibata, Kitaku,
Osaka.

Index

Numbers in italics indicate illustrations

Aberdeen 12
Aberlour *37,* 46, *69,* 93, *93,*
    94, *94, 169*
Angus 19
Ardbeg 17, 18, 94, *94*, 95, *95*
Auchentoshan 96, *96*

Balmoral 12
Balvenie 3, 34, *70, 80,* 81, 83,
    97, *97*
Bennachie 98, *98*
Benriach *34,* 98, *99*
Benromach 99
Black Bottle 88
Bladnoch 99, 100
Blair Athol 100, *100*
Bowmore 3, 17, 18, 33, 34,
    42, 55, *79,* 83, 101, *101,*
    102, 103
Bowmore Round Church 18,
    18
Bruichladdich 104
Bunnahabhain 17, 104, *105*
Burns, Robert *23,* 160, 161,
    161, 170

Caol Ila 17, 39, *45,* 84, 88,
    106, *106*
Cardhu 21, *38,* 88, 107, *107*
Chalice 23
Chariot 23, 24, 25, 26
Chivas Brothers *14*

Chivas Brothers The Century of
    Malts 108, *108*
Chivas Regal 88
Clynelish 108, 109
Cock O' The North 146
Cragganmore 109, *109,* 110
Culloden 8

Dà Mhìle *85*
Dallas Dhu 110
Daluaine 20
Dalwhinnie 82, 110, *111*
Delibes 23
Doig, Charles Chree 19
Drambuie 146, *147*
Drambuie Cream 148
Dufftown, 134, 136
Edinburgh *155, 156*
Edradour 4, 39, 59, 111, *111,*
    112

Famous Grouse 112, *113*
Ferintosh 8

Glen Elgin 21
Glen Grant 4, 116, *116*, 117,
    169
Glen Moray 83, 122, *122*
Glen Ord 122, 123, *123*
Glen Scotia 124
Glen Spey *92*
Glenfarclas 113, 114

Glenfiddich 15, 50, *81,* 84, *84,* 97, 114, *114,* 115
Glenfiddich Liqueur 148
Glengoyne 25, 116
Glenkeith 117
Glenkinchie 82, 117, 118
Glenlivet 9, 11, *11, 41,* 81, *83,* 84, 118, *118,* 119
Glenlossie 119
Glenmorangie 51, 81, 82, *82,* 83, *119, 120,* 121
Glenturret *9, 10,* 124, *124*
Golden Promise 3, 23, 24, 25, *26*
Grant, William 97, 114

Highland Park 4, 21, 33, 34, 55, 125, *125,* 126

Imperial 21
Iona 18
Islay 3, 16, 17, *17,* 18, 33, 56, 71, 79, 80, 101, 130, 166
Isle of Jura 126, 127
Isle of Mull 143
Isle of Skye *3*

James Chivas 12
Johnnie Walker 12, *87,* 144, *145*
Jura 18, *45,* 106, *106*

Kildalton Cross 18

Kilmarnock 12
Knockando 21, 127
Lagavulin 17, *40,* 82, 127, 128, *128*
Laphroaig 17, 34, 129, *129, 130*
Linkwood 130
Littlemill 131
Lochindaal 131
Longmorn 21, 48, 131

Macallan 3, 25, 55, 67, 68, 132, *132,* 133
Macdonalds 134
Melanie 26
Mortlach 134

Oban 82, 134
Old Original Oldbury Sheep Dip 135
Old Pulteney 135, 136, *136*
Optic 23
Orkney 4, 9, 33, 40, 158, 159, *159,* 164, 165, *165*

Pittyvaich 136, *137*
Poit Dhubh 137
Prisma 23

Queen Victoria 12

Rosebank 138
Royal Brackla *10,* 138
Royal Lochnagar 139, *139, 150*

St Columba 7
St Drostan 7
St Drostan's Well 93
Scapa 140
Singleton of Auchroisk 140
Springbank 34, 70, 141
Stag's Breath 149
Strathisla 21, *21*, 55, 88,
    141, 142, *142*

Talisker 3, 21, 82, 88, 142
Tankard 24
Tobermory 143
Tomatin 143, 144
Triumph 27

Wick 135

ACKNOWLEDGMENTS

The writing of this book was greatly helped by: David Robertson of The Macallan, Jim McEwan of Bruichladdich, Dr James Brosnan of The Scotch Whisky Research Institute, David Stewart and Mike Weber of Wm Grant, Steven Muller, Gordon Motion and John Ramsay of the Edrington Group, Lynne Grant of Highland Park, Jim Cryle of The Glenlivet, David Boyd of Campbell Distillers, Alan Winchester of Aberlour, John Reid of Edradour, Jim Beveridge of United Distillers & Vintners Brand Technical Centre, Ian Henderson of Laphroaig, Dr Bill Lumsden of Glenmorangie, Jurgen Deibel (Whisky Consultant), Stewart McBain, Tom Smith of Johnnie Walker, Alan Greig of Chivas Brothers, Richard Patterson of Whyte & Mackay, Aoife Martin of United Distillers & Vintners, Suntory, Springbank Distillery, Glengoyne Distillery, Isle of Jura Distillery, Robin Nicholson of the Drambuie Collection, Sir Iain Noble of Praban na Linne (The Gaelic Whisky Company), The Orkney Tourist Board, the Scottish Tourist Board, The Burns Federation, Speyside Cooperage, The Kentucky Distiller's Association, Riedel, Campbell Evans of The Scotch Whisky Association, Andrew Carney of Phipps PR, Lindsay Morgan of BMA Communications, Vanessa Wright of Campbell Distillers, and CLASS magazine.

For hosting malt whisky tastings I would like to thank: The Malt Whisky Bar at The Athenaeum

Hotel, Boisdale, The Churchill Bar & Cigar Divan at The Churchill Inter-Continental Hotel, and the Four Seasons Hotel, London.

I would like to thank the following distilleries, and the master distillers and distillery managers, for allowing me to visit and being so generous in sharing their expertise: Aberlour, The Balvenie, Bowmore, Bunnahabhain, Caol Ila, Cardhu, Cragganmore, Edradour, Glenfiddich, Glen Grant, The Glenlivet, Highland Park, Knockando, Lagavulin, Laphroaig, The Macallan, Strathisla, Talisker.

PICTURE ACKNOWLEDGMENTS

The Advertising Archives, London 92, 122
Edinburgh Photographic Library 9, 10, 153, 154, 158, 159, 161, 163
Orkney Tourist Board 157 (Alistair Smith), 165
The Public Records Office 6 (Ref. no 1/138)
The Sherry Institute in Spain. Photograph by Carlos Navajos courtesy of ICEX (Spanish Institute for Foreign Trade) 66.

With special thanks to Aberlour and Edradour, Auchentoshan, BMA Communications, The Bowmore distillery, The Chivas Brothers, The Drambuie Liquer Company Ltd., The Glenlivet distillery, Glenkinchie distillery, Kable Public Relations, The Macallan Distilleries Ltd., Phipps Public Relations Ltd, Glenmorangie plc, The Red Consultancy, Seagram Corporate Communications, United Distillers and Vintners.

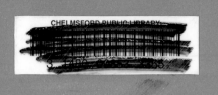